D0849513

The Sector Strategist

Founded in 1807, John Wiley & Sons is the oldest independent publishing company in the United States. With offices in North America, Europe, Australia and Asia, Wiley is globally committed to developing and marketing print and electronic products and services for our customers' professional and personal knowledge and understanding.

The Wiley Finance series contains books written specifically for finance and investment professionals as well as sophisticated individual investors and their financial advisors. Book topics range from portfolio management to e-commerce, risk management, financial engineering, valuation and financial instrument analysis, as well as much more.

For a list of available titles, please visit our web site at www.WileyFinance.com.

The Sector Strategist

Using New Asset Allocation Techniques to Reduce Risk and Improve Investment Returns

TIMOTHY J. McINTOSH

WILEY

John Wiley & Sons, Inc.

Published by John Wiley & Sons, Inc., Hoboken, New Jersey.
Published simultaneously in Canada.

For general information on our other products and services or for technical
support, please contact our Customer Care Department within the United States at
(800) 762-2974, outside the United States at (317) 572-3993 or fax (317) 572-4002.

Wiley also publishes its books in a variety of electronic formats. Some content that
appears in print may not be available in electronic books. For more information
about Wiley products, visit our web site at www.wiley.com.

Library of Congress Cataloging-in-Publication Data:

McIntosh, Timothy J.
    The sector strategist : using new asset allocation techniques to reduce risk and
improve investment returns / Timothy J. McIntosh.
        p. cm.
    Includes bibliographical references and index.
    ISBN 978-1-118-17190-5 (cloth); ISBN 978-1-118-22682-7 (ebk);
    ISBN 978-1-118-23979-7 (ebk); ISBN 978-1-118-26452-2 (ebk)
    1. Portfolio management. 2. Investments. I. Title.
    HG4529.5.M386 2012
    332.6–dc23

                                                                    2011050801

Printed in the United States of America

10 9 8 7 6 5 4 3 2 1

Contents

Introduction

The stock and bond markets have offered investors rewarding returns for the past 100 years, or what is considered the "long run". However, the long run may not be "long enough" for many investors. An individual investor has a finite period to grow investment assets, normally starting from age 35 to 65. Depending on the historical period the investor lives in, the ultimate returns on investment can be dramatically different than expectations. This is especially true if the investment growth period in question is 20 years or less. Investors in stock or equities have learned this truth if their window of opportunity was from 1929-1949 or 1964-1984. Investors in bonds also do not always escape the dreaded window of time as well. If interest rates are extremely low in the beginning time period, like 1948, then returns on bonds can also be substantially lower than the long-term averages. This problem is not just associated with stocks and bonds. Gold and commodities have suffered elongated periods of stagnated returns. Buying gold at its absolute peak in 1980 ($675) and holding it for 20 years ($284 in 2000) sure turned out to be a losing long term investment. Real estate does not always go up as several pundits argued forcefully in the mid-2000s. I expect that the real estate market will surely stagnate for another decade at a minimum based on historical precedent.

The fact is that all investment categories, or asset classes, are highly volatile over time. The most important aspect of garnering a respectable return on an investment is primarily determined by the starting date of your investment horizon and the value of the various asset classes at that point in time.

In 2012, major asset classes like stocks, bonds, real estate, gold, and commodities are either at long term averages or at a peak in value. Historically we are in a time of excess valuation that is closest to the early 1930s. Leverage is high, which will damper the future returns of real estate. Bond yields are extremely low due to excessive debt and Federal Reserve policies. Gold has returned to relative price levels last seen in the Reagan era. The best of the bunch is most likely stocks. However, when you examine the stock market based on a historical context, value is also not at the low end of the spectrum. This presents a big problem for both the individual investor and pension funds. This is due to the fact that expectations for long term returns are solidly in the 8% range. Over the last fifty years, a diversified portfolio of various assets would have provided for such a return. In the next fifty years, it is most likely that the same will occur. But, the 8% future return will most likely be back loaded. The next ten years do not offer an investor much hope to garner to same return guarantee.

This text was written to provide an alternative to traditional asset class investing and enhance the possibility of garnering an above average investment return. I begin in Chapter 1 with a description of return expectations. I discuss the history of the stock and bond markets over the past 100 years. You will learn what returns have been generated by the stock and bond markets over various periods of time. Additionally, I present the assets in a historical context, so that an investor may better understand how to better evaluate future return expectations. In Chapter 2, I present my sector strategy. I present evidence on how traditional investing and correlation has changed over the past thirty years. I discuss an alternative to traditional benchmarking to the index through sector investing. I describe the major sectors in the economy and list which sectors have not only been the best performers over time, but also the least volatile. Chapters 3, 4, 5, 6, and 7 present my recommended sectors. These are the sectors of the economy I recommend you should focus your equity investment dollars in. Each of these five chapters reviews a sector in detail including future prospects, breakdown of major companies, and rules of individual selection. I also give examples of purchases made within the sectors based on a contrarian investment strategy. Chapter 8 features the alternative investments I recommend to balance your stock portfolio. This includes corporate bonds, REITs, and precious metals. One of the most important topics, fundamental analysis, is explained in Chapter 9. You will learn some basic tools to dissect a balance sheet and income statement. I discuss the difference between growth and value investing and how to utilize relative value techniques for stock selection. Chapter 10 examines the selection process, including how many stocks and bonds you should hold. I also discuss methods to utilize my strategy through mutual funds and ETFs. I have added this chapter for those investors who are either beginners or do not have the time to select individual securities. In Chapter 11, the major components of the book are put together and several model portfolios are examined. Each portfolio is back-tested over the past 25 years. Fortunately, the last 25 years have presented investors with a multitude of different economic and market scenarios, including strong bull markets and tremendously destructive bear markets. Here is where all the research and theory come together. My recommended portfolios will look different from a financial plan you would see from a typical financial advisor or investment magazine. I believe most investment plans put together today that encompass traditional allocations to stocks and bonds won't work in meeting the needs of today's investor. In the next 11 chapters, I'll demonstrate a new investment strategy is necessary to survive and generate an above average return in the next decade.

CHAPTER 1

The Return Dilemma

Living in dreams of yesterday, we find ourselves still dreaming of impossible future conquests.

Charles Lindberg

Family Office Exchange (FOX), a leading provider of research and education to the wealthy and their advisors, released the results of a survey they made in early 2011. For 2011, wealthy families anticipated a median long-term return of 8% from their investments, consistent with previous years' studies. On the corporate side of the ledger, sentiment is equally optimistic. According to Milliman, a large independent actuarial and consulting firm, large public U.S. companies currently maintain an expected rate of return of 8% for their firms' pension funds, a slight decrease compared with 8.1% for 2009. The annual Milliman study covers 100 U.S. public companies with the largest defined benefit pension plan assets. Although the expected return has steadily declined during the past decade from a gaudy 9.4% in 2001, an 8% return expectation is still above the long-term averages.

The Milliman study also listed the percentage of pension plan assets invested in equities in 2010, which was 45%, a slight increase from the 44% in the previous year. Bond allocations were unchanged at 36%, and allocation to other investments, including cash, increased from 19% to 20% during 2010. Individual investors, who as a class are typically more aggressive, held 50.9% of their portfolios in stocks and stock funds according to the July 2011 AAII Asset Allocation Survey. This is below average given that the historical standard is for 60% of a typical portfolio to be earmarked for stocks. Bond and bond funds accounted for 25.5% of individual investor portfolios. The historical average is a surprisingly low 15%. This is no doubt due to the low returns earned on cash equivalents. In the survey, individual investors maintained a 23.6% position of their portfolio dollars in cash. The historical average is 25%. The question of all questions is Will the optimists earn the 8% expected return with those allocations? To answer this critical question, an investor must study history and make reasonable assumptions about the future.

An examination of 80 years of data shows the following results:

- The annualized return for the Standard & Poor's (S&P) 500 Index (and its precursor S&P 90 Index) between 1930 and 2010 was 9.37%.
- Dividends have been a noteworthy contributor to the total return of the S&P 500. From 1930 through 2010, dividends accounted for 43% of the S&P 500s return. The percentage contribution of dividends to the total return has been declining steadily since mid-century. During the past 20 years, dividends have accounted for only a quarter of the total return. U.S. bond market returns are lower in comparison to equities for the 80-year period starting in 1930.[1] The average return is only 5.72%.

Most investors combine investments in stocks and bonds to hopefully produce a better return with less risk. This process is known as asset allocation. The theory is that by including asset categories with investment returns that move up and down under

TABLE 1.1 Asset Allocation History, 1930–2010

		Average	
Stocks/Bonds	Average Return	Frequency of losing years	Worst Return
100% Stock, 0% Bond	9.37%	28%	−55.1%
80% Stock, 20% Bond	8.62%	26%	−39.9%
60% Stock, 40% Bond	7.91%	24%	−27.6%
50% Stock, 50% Bond	7.65%	21%	−18.8%

Source: Roger G. Ibbottson and Rex A. Sinquefield, "Stocks, Bonds, Bills, and Inflation: Year-by-Year Historical Returns," *Journal of Business,* University of Chicago Press, 2011.

different market conditions within a total portfolio, an investor can potentially enhance return while reducing risk. Historically, the returns of the two major asset categories such as stocks and bonds have not moved up and down at the same time. If one asset is producing losses, such as stocks in 2008, other assets will rise in value to offset your losses. Table 1.1 shows the breakdown of the long-term returns of combining the two assets.

Most individual investors and pension funds would be happy with these long-term return scenarios. However, three key elements have a dramatic impact on whether or not these returns can be realized:

- The current price-to-earnings (P/E) ratio of the market
- The current dividend yield of the market
- The current bond yield of the market

Importance of the P/E ratio

According to the Wall Street Journal, the P/E ratio of the S&P 500 Index at the end of 2011, based on earnings over the past 12 months, was approximately 15. The average P/E ratio of the

S&P 500 Index and other large-cap stocks over the past 80 years
has been approximately 16, based on 12-month trailing earnings. P/E, of course, stands for price/earnings, and it is one of
the essential tools investors use to estimate value when it comes
to stock analysis. The price/earnings ratio is one of the oldest
and most frequently used metrics. Here is the formula;

$$price/earnings = price\ of\ share\ of\ stock/E.P.S.$$
$$(Earnings\ per\ Share)$$

The P/E ratio gives you an indication of a stock's value. If it
is low (though some sectors tend to be chronically low) it usually means that the stock price reflects a reasonable valuation
relative to the earnings stream. If it is high (though some sectors
tend to be chronically high) it usually means that the stock price
reflects a high valuation relative to the earnings stream. Most of
the time the P/E is calculated using E.P.S from the last four quarters. This is also known as the trailing P/E. However, it can also
be utilized by estimating the E.P.S. figure expected over the next
four quarters. This is known as the leading or forward P/E. A
third variation is sometimes used that consists of the past two
quarters and estimates of the next two quarters. There is not a
huge difference between these variations. It is important you realize that you are using actual historical data for the calculation
in the first case. The other two are based on analyst estimates
that are not always perfect or precise. My preference has always
been on trailing P/E.

The P/E ratio is a much better indicator of the value of a
stock than the market price alone. For example, all things being
equal, a $10 stock with a P/E of 75 is much more expensive than
a $100 stock with a P/E of 20. Therefore, the P/E ratio allows you
to compare two different companies with two different market
prices—comparing "apples to apples," so to speak. A potential
problem with the P/E involves companies that are not profitable
and consequently have a negative E.P.S. There are varying

opinions on how to deal with this. I recommend that if a firm does not have a P/E due to depressed earnings, an investor should use an alternative valuation model, such as the Price/Sales ratio. It is difficult to state whether a particular P/E is high or low without taking into account two main factors:

Company Growth Rates

A P/E is based primarily on the growth rate of companies within the index. Generally, the higher the growth rate, the higher the expected P/E. If the projected growth rate does not justify the P/E, the market might be overpriced.

The average P/E ratio at the end of each year for the overall market, based on trailing four quarter numbers, is shown in Table 1.2. The far-right column gives the average 10-year future total return of the market on an annualized basis. Figure 1.1 shows the rolling returns on a 10-year basis.

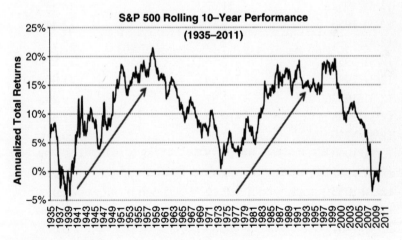

FIGURE 1.1 Rolling Returns on a 10-Year Basis

Source: Roger G. Ibbottson and Rex A. Sinquefield, "Stocks, Bonds, Bills, and Inflation: Year-by-Year Historical Returns," *Journal of Business*, University of Chicago Press, 2011.

TABLE 1.2 Average P/E Ratio for Overall Market

	Period P/E	Forward 10-Year Annualized Return
12/31/1936	16.84	8.42%
12/31/1937	19.34	4.41%
12/31/1938	20.64	9.62%
12/31/1939	13.88	7.26%
12/31/1940	10.08	9.17%
12/31/1941	7.49	13.38%
12/31/1942	9.49	17.28%
12/31/1943	12.41	17.07%
12/31/1944	14.28	14.31%
12/31/1945	18.08	17.12%
12/31/1946	14.43	16.69%
12/31/1947	9.50	18.43%
12/31/1948	6.64	16.44%
12/31/1949	7.22	20.06%
12/31/1950	7.19	19.35%
12/31/1951	9.74	16.16%
12/31/1952	11.07	16.43%
12/31/1953	9.88	13.44%
12/31/1954	12.99	15.91%
12/31/1955	12.56	12.82%
12/31/1956	13.69	11.06%
12/31/1957	11.87	9.20%
12/31/1958	19.10	12.85%
12/31/1959	17.67	10.01%
12/31/1960	17.77	7.81%
12/31/1961	22.43	8.18%
12/31/1962	17.19	7.06%
12/31/1963	18.66	9.93%
12/31/1964	18.63	6.01%
12/31/1965	17.81	1.24%
12/31/1966	14.47	3.27%
12/31/1967	18.10	6.63%
12/31/1968	18.03	3.59%

12/31/1969	15.93	3.16%
12/31/1970	17.96	5.86%
12/31/1971	17.91	8.44%
12/31/1972	18.39	6.47%
12/31/1973	11.95	6.68%
12/31/1974	7.71	10.61%
12/31/1975	11.33	14.76%
12/31/1976	10.84	14.33%
12/31/1977	8.73	13.82%
12/31/1978	7.79	15.26%
12/31/1979	7.26	16.33%
12/31/1980	9.16	17.55%
12/31/1981	7.98	13.93%
12/31/1982	11.13	17.59%
12/31/1983	11.76	16.19%
12/31/1984	10.05	14.94%
12/31/1985	14.46	14.40%
12/31/1986	16.72	14.84%
12/31/1987	14.12	15.28%
12/31/1988	11.69	18.05%
12/31/1989	15.45	19.18%
12/31/1990	15.47	18.20%
12/31/1991	28.12	17.46%
12/31/1992	22.82	12.93%
12/31/1993	21.31	9.33%
12/31/1994	15.01	11.06%
12/31/1995	18.14	12.07%
12/31/1996	19.13	9.08%
12/31/1997	24.43	8.42%
12/31/1998	32.60	5.91%
12/31/1999	30.50	−1.38%
12/31/2000	26.41	−0.95%
12/31/2001	46.50	1.41%
12/31/2002	31.89	?
12/31/2003	22.81	?
12/31/2004	20.70	?

(*continued*)

TABLE 1.2 (*Continued*)

	Period P/E	Forward 10-Year Annualized Return
12/30/2005	17.85	?
12/31/2006	17.40	?
12/31/2007	22.19	?
12/31/2008	40.70	?
12/31/2009	34.94	?
12/31/2010	17.23	?

Source for P/E ratios: Standard & Poor's.
Source for return data: Roger G. Ibbottson and Rex A. Sinquefield, "Stocks, Bonds, Bills, and Inflation: Year-by-Year Historical Returns," *Journal of Business,* University of Chicago Press, 2011.

Here is the performance of the S&P 500 from the lowest 10 P/E ratio starting points, versus the highest P/E ratio starting points. See Table 1.3

TABLE 1.3 Lowest/Highest P/E Starting Points

Lowest P/E Starting Points

	Period P/E	Forward 10-Year Annualized Return
12/31/1948	6.64	16.44%
12/31/1950	7.19	19.35%
12/31/1949	7.22	20.06%
12/31/1979	7.26	16.33%
12/31/1941	7.49	13.38%
12/31/1974	7.71	10.61%
12/31/1978	7.79	15.26%
12/31/1981	7.98	13.93%
12/31/1977	8.73	13.82%
12/31/1980	9.16	17.55%
Averages	7.71	15.67%

Highest P/E Starting Points

	Period P/E	Forward 10-Year Annualized Return
12/31/2001	46.51	1.41%
12/31/1998	32.64	5.91%
12/31/1999	30.55	−1.38%
12/31/1991*	28.12	17.46%
12/31/2000	26.41	−0.95%
12/31/1997	24.43	8.42%
12/31/1992	22.82	12.93%
12/31/1961	22.43	8.18%
12/31/1993	21.31	9.33%
12/31/1938	20.64	9.62%
Averages	27.57	7.09%

Source for P/E ratios: Standard & Poor's.

Source for return data: Roger G. Ibbottson and Rex A. Sinquefield, "Stocks, Bonds, Bills, and Inflation: Year-by-Year Historical Returns," *Journal of Business*, University of Chicago Press, 2011.

Conclusions about P/E Ratios and Subsequent Returns

In predicting future returns for the stock market, P/E ratio should be your primary indicator. Here are eight key facts regarding this most critical statistic:

1. For the overall stock market, P/E is the major driver of whether returns will most likely be above or below average in future periods.
2. In general, the lower the market P/E ratio, the higher the subsequent 10-year average return.
3. When average P/E ratios are below 10 for the market as a whole, subsequent 10-year average returns are well above the standard.
4. The stock market can advance strongly through a combination of higher earnings and low starting P/E ratio. P/E ratio

multiple expansion is a critical component in future returns being above the long-term averages.

5. During recessions, earnings for the S&P 500 companies can collapse, thus leading to a high P/E ratio based on trailing earnings. This could indicate an overvalued market based solely on P/E ratio. In this case, an investor may use a forward P/E ratio as a secondary indicator. In the preceding chart, 1991 is a good example.

6. A high trailing P/E ratio does not guarantee that future returns will be below average for the next year, or even the next five years. The shorter term predictability of high P/E ratios on future returns is poor.

7. Higher inflation causes lower P/Es and deflation causes lower P/Es; P/Es generally peak at higher levels when inflation is low and stable.

8. In addition to higher starting P/E ratios, higher starting profit margins have a negative impact on future expected returns.

Other Valuation Models

The foregoing P/E model utilized to forecast future returns has been criticized in some circles because of the limited nature of such a basic model. Other more sophisticated valuation models have been utilized by various managers to better hypothesize future returns including the Q ratio and the Shiller model. In addition, many analysts also use other factors along with the P/E ratios, including adjustments for profit margins and inflation considerations.

Q RATIO   The Q ratio was developed in 1969 by the late economist and Nobel laureate James Tobin. The Tobin Q measures the market value of a company (i.e., its stock price) relative to the replacement cost of its assets. More recently, the ratio has been promoted by Stephen Wright and Andrew Smithers in the book

Valuing Wall Street. The Q ratio is the total price of the market divided by the replacement cost of all its companies. The Q ratio contrasts the total value of the stock market with the net replacement cost of corporate assets. When stock market prices are above asset values, an investor should buy an asset through direct purchase, rather than through equities. A Q value greater than one indicates that a company's assets could be purchased more cheaply than the company itself and consequently, the market is overvaluing the firm in question. A Q ratio of less than one indicates market undervaluation. Wright and Smithers found that a high Tobin's Q for the nonfinancial equities in the S&P 500 accurately predicts a future low real rate of return from investing in the S&P 500 Index. The team argued that in time arbitrage would ultimately drive the value of the private and public markets together.

Academic research has placed a high value on the predictive capability of the Q ratio. In a paper written for the *Journal of Investing* in 2002 by Edward Tower and Matthew Harney from Duke University,[2] the Q ratio demonstrated strong predictive power. Their results suggested the Q ratio provided the most compelling value of the alternatives they tested, including several P/E models. Tower and Harney tested the Q ratio against P/E ratios using 30-, 20-, 10-, and 1-year moving-averaged earnings. The team then ranked the predictive capacity to succeeding rates of return on the S&P 500 index. They then categorized the outcomes by R-squared (represents the percentage of a fund or security's movements that can be explained by movements in a benchmark index).

The Q ratio had the top score in regard to predictive power. The P/E ratio categories (30-, 20-, 10-, 1-year) offered secondary predictive value, in order of the length of time period. Since 1900, the average Q ratio has been 0.78. The ratio has had a wide range for the period, hitting all-time lows twice, in 1948 and 1974 (0.3). The high point in history came in year 2000, when the ratio hit 1.88. As recently as March 2009, the ratio once again had dropped to 0.43, offering a compelling buying opportunity versus the long-term averages. There have been noted criticisms of the Q ratio. In calculating the Q ratio, book value minus intangible assets is utilized. Thus the denominator excludes intangible assets. Intangible assets (e.g., patents, trademarks, brand recognition, license agreements, and trade secrets) are increasingly important in the economy of the 21st century.

Professor Robert E. Hall of Stanford University published a paper on the stock market and capital accumulation in the *American Economic Review* in 2001.[3] He found that intangible assets do play a larger role and that the accumulation of intangible capital had been much faster in the previous decade. A new paper released in 2010 evaluated the Q ratio with the addition of intangible assets.[4] Professors Erica Li of the University of Michigan and Laura Liu of the Hong Kong University of Science and Technology found that adding intangible assets to Tobin's Q explained stock returns significantly better than the Q theory that maintained only tangible assets. The authors Li and Liu also found that intangible assets are more crucial for firms to sustain their comparative advantages than tangible assets because it is more costly to accumulate intangible assets rapidly. Furthermore, they found that it is advantageous for a company to consistently invest in intangible assets. Considering the growing impact of intangibles on the Q ratio, the long-term range of .3 to 1.88 might no longer be as germane as history suggests. The current Q ratio as of August 2011 is well over 1, suggesting a stretched overvaluation of the markets. However, based on trailing P/E ratio mechanism, the stock market was trading at only 13 times trailing earnings, indicating longer investment horizon value. Overall, the Q ratio has merit based on its strong predictive value. However, consideration must be given to the increasing importance of intangibles in calculating the Q ratio.

THE SHILLER P/E METHOD   Robert Shiller from Yale University has developed a separate, widely followed P/E model. Shiller has postulated that utilizing a longer-term cyclical P/E ratio is a better methodology. In this manner, an investor will not be misled by earnings at the top or bottom of economic cycles. Shiller thus smoothes earnings by calculating average earnings over the previous 10 years. He measures this as the cyclically adjusted price earnings ratio.

The inherent problem with Shiller's approach is that there are no assurances that average earnings will end up estimating normalized earnings. If earnings are elevated over a previous 10-year period, an analyst will end up with a higher than average normalized estimate. The reverse is also true. David Bianco, Chief U.S. Market Strategist at Merrill Lynch, has also recently questioned the utility of the Shiller P/E. Mr. Bianco found the 2011 Shiller P/E of 24 was 50% above its 1900–2010 average. The problem was Dr. Shiller's estimate of earnings, at only $55 on an inflation adjusted ten-year trailing average. Comparing this to the average 2011 estimate of traditional analysts of nearly $100 for the S&P 500, Dr. Shiller's average substantially discounts current earnings. I find Dr. Shiller's model, although theoretically correct, not as useful as traditional P/E models or the Q ratio.

CORPORATE PROFIT MARGIN ANALYSIS   Since 1948, net corporate profit margins for the S&P 500 corporations have ranged from just above 4% to nearly 10%. Net profit margin is calculated by dividing net profits by net revenues and is generally stated as a percentage. The net profit margin is a signal of how efficient a firm is at producing a profit after all costs have been factored in. The higher the net profit margin, the more successful the firm is at turning total revenue into actual profits. I prefer the net profit margin to other profitability ratios because it takes in all factors in a corporation. It not only measures how well the firm can control expenses at the cost of goods sold level (gross margin) and how well a firm manages its operating costs (operating margin) but also factors in the firm's interest on debt and tax structure. Net profit margins allow an analyst both to compare firms within similar sectors and to gauge which sectors and/or industries are most profitable. Profitability has risen and dropped rapidly depending on the economic environment and the individual standing of the corporation. From 1950 to 1965, profitability remained extremely elevated (6–10%) due to the economic boom that followed World War II. Net profit margins then peaked during the mid-1960s and declined substantially throughout the 1970s. The period of the 1970s was one of very high inflation, uncertain economic policies, oil embargoes, and labor unrest. In the mid-1980s, margins continued to decline, although at a more level pace, ultimately hitting a low of 4% in the recession of 1991. Average net margins for the S&P 500 doubled over the following decade, reaching a high of 8.1% in 2001. Margins rose until the financial crash of 2008, after which margins once again dropped to the 4% level.

Do margins foretell future equity returns? The answer is mixed. A low net margin starting point, such as the 4% level, does indicate a floor in equity pricing. In the two years since 1948 the net margin level hit 4% (1991, 2008), both offered investors a great buying entry point. However, during the early 1950s, net margins were above 8% and subsequent short-term and longer-term stock returns were excellent. Blackrock Corporation recently reported in an updated paper[5] that the likelihood that margin trends, in isolation, are not an effective tool for forecasting market returns is limited. Blackrock pointed to evidence that of eight post-war peaks in the S&P 500, only two actually correlated with peaks in corporate margins.

Importance of Dividends in Total Returns

As mentioned previously, from 1930 through 2010 dividends accounted for 43 percent of the S&P 500s return. Table 1.4

TABLE 1.4 Return from Dividends

Period	Average Annual Return	Dividend Contribution
1930s	0.30%	NM
1940s	8.90%	66.7%
1950s	19.2%	29.3%
1960s	7.7%	43.1%
1970s	5.7%	72.1%
1980s	17.4%	27.5%
1990s	18.1%	12.9%
2000s	−1.0%	NM

Source: Ned Davis Research.

shows the percentage of return from dividends for each decade since 1930.

As the dividend contribution declined over time as a percentage of total return, the payout ratio for companies has also declined. Table 1.5 shows the payout ratio for companies over the preceding 80 years.

In 1973, 52.8 percent of publicly traded nonfinancial firms paid dividends.[6] The percentage of payers rose to a peak of 66.5

TABLE 1.5 Payout Ratio

Period	Average Payout Ratio	Average Dividend Market Yield
1930s	90.1%	5.9%
1940s	59.4%	6.8%
1950s	54.6%	5.1%
1960s	56.0%	3.1%
1970s	45.5%	5.2%
1980s	48.6%	4.5%
1990s	47.6%	2.8%
2000s	39.0%	2.6%

Source: Ned Davis Research.

in 1978. It then fell dramatically throughout the boom years of the 1980s and 1990s. By 1999, only 20.8 percent of firms paid annual dividends. From 1973 to 1977, one-third of newly listed firms paid dividends. In 1999, only 3.7% of new listings paid dividends. Dr. Eugene Fama and Kenneth French postulated that the decline in the incidence of dividend payers over this period was due to an increasing tilt of new publicly traded firms that were more growth oriented within new industries. These firms had the following characteristics: small size, low earnings, and large investments relative to earnings; they generally paid low or nil dividends. This is a far cry from the days after the Great Depression. During the late 1930s and 1940s, dividends were widely distributed among public companies; they were considered a key source of income and were utilized as an important tool to assure safety.

Investors that experienced the great losses resulting from the 1929 crash demanded higher dividends. In fact, the average dividend yield on stocks exceeded 20-year Treasury Bond yields through 1957. The number of companies issuing dividends today has diminished over time as new industries have emerged (e.g., information technology, biotechnology) that would rather reinvest their own capital. But dividends are a large part of total return for the market and also protect investor capital during poor market environments. For example, during the "lost decade" of the 2000s, the S&P 500 Index declined −2.3% due to price depreciation, but the income provided by dividends (1.8 percentage points) minimized the losses, resulting in a less painful −0.5% total return throughout the decade. Investors that concentrated investment dollars in high-dividend firms did even better.

Inflation can also have a dramatic impact on stock returns. The decade of the 1970s provides an example of how inflation has impacted returns for stocks. During the 7-year period from 1974 to 1980, the average rate of inflation was 9.3% while the S&P 500 Index had an average annual return of 9.9%, with dividend income accounting for nearly half of the total return.

Academic studies have demonstrated that the average dividend yield of the market also has an impact on future returns of the market. Studies done by prominent researchers such as Fama and French (1988) and Campbell and Shiller (1998)[7] concluded that today's dividend yield has the capacity to predict multi-year stock market returns. More recently, Professor John Cochrane from the University of Chicago[8] found that when market prices are low relative to dividends, subsequent 7-year returns are likely to be higher than average. Consider the top line in Figure 1.2 from Dr. Cochrane, which depicts the dividend/price ratio for NYSE stocks, alongside the future 7-year returns. The correlation between the two lines is very high. This same pattern also appears in P/E ratios as discussed previously. One caveat is that all the authors found that stock returns are predictable only when measured over several years. Short-term predictive ability of the dividend model is also weak. Thus a low

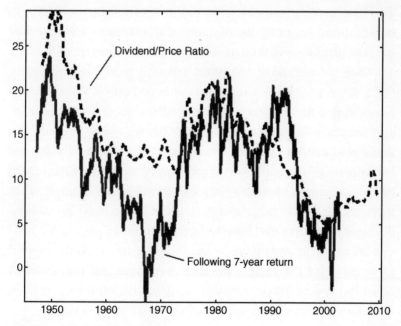

FIGURE 1.2 No Random Walk
Source: John H. Cochrane, University of Chicago.

average dividend yield in one year does not have much predictive power for determining the following year's return.

Importance of the Bond Yields

The average bond total return since 1930 is 5.82%. However, as with stocks, the returns are highly unstable. Bond returns are most dependent on the starting interest rate and the changes in general interest rates over time—that is, when interest rates increase, the value of bonds decrease and vice versa. This fact may have a dramatic impact on future expected returns. Throughout the Great Depression of 1929–1933, bond yields declined as economic growth and inflation turned negative. Under the New Deal in the 1930s, the U.S. Treasury issued new bonds at low interest rates to fund public works and America's preparation for and entry into World War II. This kept yields in check for the decade. The 10-year U.S. Treasury yield was at 3.29% at the start of 1930 but declined to 2.21% by the end of the decade. Interest plus gains in price appreciation resulted in a total return of 4.48%.

Over the decade of the 1940s, inflation picked up, averaging 6.1%, while 10-year Treasury yields averaged only 2.33%. The total return during the 1940s was a mere 1.82%, a quote below the average rate of inflation. During the 1950s, economic growth was strong and interest rates began to slowly climb higher. By the end of the decade, 10-year U.S. Treasuries were yielding 4.72%. In fact, the 40 year period from 1940 to 1979 provides an example of an extended stage of rising bond yields. As discussed previously, changes in yields have a hefty impact on bond prices. As bond yields first rise in a low–interest rate environment, capital losses are more pronounced because lower interest payments only partially offset the capital losses. As yields increase, higher annual interest payments are more successful in offsetting the price declines.

This latter concept was demonstrated in the 1970s. In the 1970s, bond yields and inflation both increased dramatically.

Yields on 10-year Treasury Bonds increased from 7.79% in 1970 to 10.8% by 1980. The annualized return for the decade was an above-average 6.97%. However, much of the return earned from interest was offset by price loss due to increasing inflation. Inflation averaged 7.8% during the 10-year period. Again the return consists of a capital loss of 4.5% offset by interest earned of 10.5%.

The 1970s marked the end of rising interest rates and led to one of the great bull markets in history. Federal Reserve Chairman Paul Volcker raised interest rates to as high as 20 percent to tame inflation during 1981. In the years that followed, inflation and interest rates declined rapidly, pushing up bond prices. The 10-year Treasury yield, which reached a high of 15.8 percent in September 1981, fell to as low as 2.05 percent on Dec. 30, 2008. Investors reaped the rewards, getting both interest alongside capital appreciation from declining bond yields. The average annual gain for 10-year Treasury Bonds was 10.36% throughout the 1980s. For the 1990s, the annualized return was 7.53%. The return over the previous decade matched the long-term average, at 5.7%. Today, the 10-year Treasury Bond is yielding below 2%. Thus after five decades, we have returned to an interest rate period similar to that of the mid-1940s.

Most of the longer-term returns from bonds over the preceding 80 years have come from the 4-decade period from 1960 to 2000. It is during this time phase that bonds provided a higher than average yield component. Combined with the capital appreciation factor from declining yields during the 1980s, bonds produced outsized returns for investors for nearly half a century.

Gazing into the Future

Given that government bond yields today are at historical lows, the opportunity for price appreciation is minimal. More likely, the collection of interest payments will provide most, if not all, of market returns. Additionally, interest rates could also trend up over the ensuing decade. This would result in capital losses as bond prices rise, reducing total return further. Much like the decade of the 1940s, total returns from bonds will most likely be subdued as either market interest rates remain constant or interest rates trend upwards. Most certainly investors cannot expect an average long-term return of 5.72%. A 3% total return over the ensuing decade is most probable. The problem with this examination is that most individual investors and pension plans have a substantial portion of their assets in bonds, especially in government bonds. As the average total portfolio return target is 8% on an annualized basis, investors must expect either a substantial decline in interest rates from the current historic lows or that equities will make up the difference.

Given that future prospects for the bond market are low, stock returns should be more constructive. The ultimate drivers of stock returns will be affected by four major components: starting P/E ratio, future earnings growth, dividend yield, and corporate profit margins. P/E ratio expansion and contraction will have a profound impact on the future returns of the market. Profit margin expansion and contraction are also constituents in forecasting future returns.

Inspecting historical data on the market, the current P/E ratio of 15 is slightly below the median. I pulled up 10 similar periods of temperate P/E ratios since 1930 as shown in Table 1.6.

Based on this analysis, at an average P/E ratio of 15, the market has historically delivered an annualized return of just above 13% per year for a 10-year period, above the historical average. Adding the historical net profit margin (since 1948) to the same chart, the results are shown in Table 1.7.

Note that when the net profit margin was at 8.9 at the end of 1966, forward returns were less favorable. This is due to the fact that although the P/E ratio was fairly moderate in 1966, average S&P 500 profit margins were elevated. Over the ensuing decade,

TABLE 1.6 Historical Market Data, P/E Ratios

	Period P/E	Forward 10-Year Annualized Return
12/31/1987	14.12	15.28%
12/31/1944	14.28	14.31%
12/31/1946	14.43	16.69%
12/31/1985	14.46	14.40%
12/31/1966	14.47	3.27%
12/31/1994	15.01	11.06%
12/31/1989	15.45	19.18%
12/31/1990	15.47	18.20%
12/31/1969	15.93	3.16%
12/31/1986	16.72	14.84%
Averages	15.03	13.04%

Source for P/E ratios: Standard & Poor's.
Source for return data: Roger G. Ibbottson and Rex A. Sinquefield, "Stocks, Bonds, Bills, and Inflation: Year-by-Year Historical Returns," *Journal of Business,* University of Chicago Press, 2011.

TABLE 1.7 Historical Market Data, P/E Ratios, Plus Net Profit Margin since 1948

	Period P/E	Net Profit	Forward 10-Year Annualized Return
12/31/1987	14.12	4.4	15.28%
12/31/1985	14.46	5.2	14.40%
12/31/1966	14.47	8.9	3.27%
12/31/1994	15.01	5.5	11.06%
12/31/1989	15.45	6.1	19.18%
12/31/1990	15.47	4.3	18.20%
12/31/1969	15.93	6.6	3.16%
12/31/1986	16.72	4.8	14.84%
Averages	15.03	5.7	13.04%

Source for P/E ratios: Standard & Poor's.
Source for return data: Roger G. Ibbottson and Rex A. Sinquefield, "Stocks, Bonds, Bills, and Inflation: Year-by-Year Historical Returns," *Journal of Business,* University of Chicago Press, 2011.

the average net profit margin dropped from 8.9 to 5.7. Thus, profit margin compression had an impact on future returns for the period from 1966 to 1975. However, also note that the future returns for the decade after 1989 (when the average profit margin was a more elevated 6.1) outperformed the 10-year period following 1990 (19.18% versus 18.20%). Therefore, there is no guarantee that the lowest average profit margin statistic will offer the highest period return. The key question is whether or not there is substantial room for net profit margins to expand. In the case of both 1989 and 1990, expansion was potentially available.

In the middle of 2011, the average net profit margin for the S&P 500 was 7.4%. This is towards the higher range witnessed in the past six decades. Listed are the three closest yearly matches in regard to P/E ratio and net profit margin, with forward 10-year average return as shown in Table 1.8.

The returns vary widely in all three instances. The average 10-year forward return is 9.7%, nearly in line with the long-term return of stocks. Given the expansive range of returns in the three closest yearly matches, a further analysis is warranted to produce a more narrow and realistic outcome. (See Table 1.9.)

To predict future returns for equities for the next ten years, an additional data piece is needed; future E.P.S. for the year 2021. Based upon data from Robert Schiller, the historical

TABLE 1.8 Three Yearly Matches, P/E Ratio, and Net Profit Margin

	Period P/E	Net Profit	Forward 10-Year Annualized Return
12/31/1954	12.99	7.7	15.91%
12/31/1959	17.67	7.9	10.01%
12/31/1969	15.93	7.1	3.16%

Source for P/E ratios: Standard & Poor's.
Source for return data: Roger G. Ibbottson and Rex A. Sinquefield, "Stocks, Bonds, Bills, and Inflation: Year-by-Year Historical Returns," *Journal of Business*, University of Chicago Press, 2011.

TABLE 1.9 Starting P/E Ratio of 15/Starting Net Profit Margin of 7.2.

Period	Current P/E	Current Net Profit	Forward
7/31/2011 to 7/31/2021	14.89	7.2	?

Source for P/E ratios: Standard & Poor's.
Source for return data: Roger G. Ibbottson and Rex A. Sinquefield, "Stocks, Bonds, Bills, and Inflation: Year-by-Year Historical Returns," *Journal of Business*, University of Chicago Press, 2011.

annualized growth rate in earnings is approximately 5.4 percent per year. For year-end 2011, Standard & Poor's has estimated $98.04 for combined S&P 500 company earnings. Given the current E.P.S., here are three possible outcomes:

Scenario #1—Expansion
1. P/E Ratio expands to 20
2. Net Profit Margins remains at 7.2%
3. Dividend Yield average expands to 3.5%
4. E.P.S. Growth averages 6%

Year	E.P.S.	Annual Price % Return	Dividend % Return	Average Yearly Return
2021	$175.50	12.3%	3.5%	15.8%

Scenario #2—Moderate
1. P/E Ratio remains at 15
2. Net Profit Margins drop to 6%
3. Dividend Yield average rises to 2.5%
4. E.P.S. Growth averages 5.4%

Year	E.P.S. (discounted for net profit margin contraction)	Annual Price % Return	Dividend % Return	Average Yearly Return
2021	$144.31	6.52%	2.5%	9.02%

Scenario #3—Contraction

1. P/E Ratio drops to 10
2. Net Profit Margins drop to 5.5%
3. Dividend Yield average remains at 2%
4. E.P.S. Growth averages 5%

Year	E.P.S. (discounted for net profit margin contraction)	Annual Price % Return	Dividend % Return	Average Yearly Return
2021	$123.20	0.69%	2%	2.69%

Based upon this analysis, expectations for stocks for the next decade still have a wide range of outcomes. It also is dependent on earnings and profit margin stability or expansion. Additionally the Q ratio, which is also useful as a secondary indicator, was at a 1.2 level during the summer of 2011. This is also close to the high range in history. Given these facts and the history of mean reversion in secular bear markets, here is my probability analysis of expected returns:

	Probability Analysis of Returns		
	Return	Probability	Result
Scenario #1	15.8%	15%	2.30%
Scenario #2	9.02%	50%	4.51%
Scenario #3	2.69%	35%	0.94%
Expectation		100%	7.75%

Given the preceding data, my expectation is that stocks will deliver a 7.75% annualized return over the next ten years. Combined with my 3% expected return from U.S. Treasury Bonds, a total portfolio return of 5% to 6% would be the most likely outcome. Thus, individual and pension fund investors, based on historical analysis, will not be able to secure expected returns utilizing the current investment strategy of focusing primary dollars on traditional investment choices.

CHAPTER 2

Sector Allocations

The only new thing in the world is the history you don't know.

Harry S. Truman

T he average 7.75% expected 10-year annual return for equities forecast in Chapter 1 is based on investments in large-cap companies through the S&P 500 stock index. To increase the odds of outperforming, an erudite investor would examine all investments within this universe to potentially secure a higher average return. I believe that by utilizing sector investment strategies, an investor can gain a competitive edge over the masses.

Fidelity Investments is generally considered the first money management firm to promote sector investing. In 1981, Fidelity launched a supply of sector mutual funds (titled the "Select" series). Fidelity launched five unique sector funds focusing concentration on the health care, energy, technology, financials, and utility sectors. The firm followed this launch in 1985 with 14 additional sector funds. Although these offerings were popular with a small portion of the investor public, the modern era of sector investing began in 1998, with the launch of the Select Sector SPDR ETFs. The Select Sector SPDRs were the first ETFs to break into the mainstream marketplace, and all of the S&P 500 stocks were divided into nine sectors. The Select Sector SPDRs allowed investors to fine-tune their sector exposure to the U.S. market at a level never seen before and quickly became the established standard for accessing specific sectors of the market. In 1999, Standard & Poor's and Morgan Stanley Capital International (MSCI) teamed up to launch the Global Industry Classification Standard (GICS), taking the sector concept already implemented in the SPDRs to a global scale. GICS became the first broadly accepted system that broke down virtually all globally listed public companies—over 38,000 in total—into a single coherent, non-overlapping sector structure.

Much of the movement to create sector-specific funds and new classifications is based on interest in finding new investment strategies, spurred in most part by new academic studies in the field. Historically, sectors have been thought to be relatively less important than other considerations in analyzing stock returns. The most prominent studies demonstrating sector unimportance were published in the 1970s. In his seminal research on the gains derived from international diversification, Bruno Solnik (1974)[1] demonstrated that diversification across the various developed countries provides greater risk reduction than diversification across the major sectors of an economy. Donald Lessard (1974, 1976)[2] confirmed Solnik's results, suggesting that country factors were the dominant drivers in security price returns. Accepting these conclusions, traditional financial planners and investment managers have adopted country selection as a critical tactical decision factor for international investments. However, beginning at the end of the 20th century, some academic studies that were published alongside the launch of the SPDR funds put those former findings in doubt.

A year 2000 study[3] performed by Brinson Partners in association with Duke University examined a factor model for 21 countries that comprise the current MSCI World Developed Markets universe. The study covered 21 developed equity markets for the period December 1985 through November 1999. Their results concluded that sectors had become an increasingly important component of security returns. More importantly, diversification across sectors actually provides greater risk reduction benefits than diversification across countries. Brinson also commented that given the increasing geographical integration of markets, they expected these phenomena to persist and even to strengthen. Their primary determinant in this sea change was globalization. The Vanguard[4] Group, Inc. has also examined sector influences for the developed markets, focusing on the period 2003–2008. Vanguard found that sector diversification produced the potential for more risk reduction benefits than did country diversification. They furthermore indicated that global sectors have become much more significant determinants of equity returns, especially for multinational companies and for companies in the developed markets of North America and Europe, as shown in Table 2.1.

The Brinson and Vanguard studies are not the only ones that confirm the altering landscape in sector investing. Recent research published by Goldman Sachs reviewed the significance of sectors. Their study demonstrated that the effect of global sector movements on individual stocks now outweighs the effect of local market influences (see Table 2.1). In January 1995, global sector influences accounted for just 7% of individual stock performance around the world. Local market influences accounted for 23%, and the global market factor for 16%. The remaining

TABLE 2.1 Influence of Stock Performance

	Jan-95	Jun-08
Company specific	54%	52%
Global sector influence	7%	18%
Local market influence	23%	15%
Global market influence	16%	15%

Source: Goldman Sachs Research, August 2008.

54% of stock variation could be put down to factors affecting specific companies.

But by mid-2008, the global sector effect had increased to 18% and was more important than either the local market (15%) or global market (15%) effects. The stock-specific influence has stayed at the same level (52%). This clearly demonstrates that a company's sector has become more important to its performance than the stock market of the country in which it is based. As trade barriers have fallen, economies have become more global, and company performance has become increasingly dependent on sector performance, rather than on geographic location.

International Investing

While research has confirmed that sector-related factors have become more important to building a diversified portfolio, traditional asset allocation techniques are becoming increasingly irrelevant. New research produced in the past decade has validated that the traditional approach of adding foreign assets to a U.S.-based portfolio is now open to discussion. This has not always been the case. Early academic studies that examined correlations (the degree to which two or more measurements on the same group of elements demonstrate the tendency to vary together) of U.S. and international markets in the 1970s and early 1980s demonstrated that international stocks had consistently low correlations. However, pundits began to question this benefit starting in the beginning of the 21st century. One of the first studies that questioned the benefits of international investing was performed by Andrew West, who published an article on the subject in *Capitalism Magazine*.[5] He examined the relationship of U.S. and international stocks for the 3-year period between 12/97 and 12/00. He concluded that the correlation between the S&P 500 stock index and the international EAFE stock index had risen to 77%, as shown in Table 2.2.

TABLE 2.2 Correlation of Monthly Returns: S&P 500 vs. EAFE

Total Correlation: 1970–2009	0.59
Correlation: 1970–1979	0.50
Correlation: 1980–1989	0.47
Correlation: 1990–1999	0.54
Correlation: 2000–2009	0.82

Source: Ibbottson.

This was quite a change from earlier time periods. The data in Table 2.2 from Ibbottson indicates the disquieting movements in correlation over the preceding four decades. Starting with a correlation of around 50% in the 1970s, correlations remained low in the 1980s and 1990s. But Andrew West's article confirmed that correlations were rising by substantial levels by the late 1990s. Not only did global equity correlations rise during the late 20th century, low historical correlations tended to mask the inefficiency of international stock diversification. An examination of the two most recent bear markets reveals that foreign stocks have not provided help during periods of stock market turbulence. For example, a portfolio fully invested in the S&P 500 Index would have lost 45% from September 2000 to September 2002. If an investor had maintained a 30% exposure to the international stock index (EAFE) along with 70% invested in the S&P 500, the loss would have been 44%. The same applies for the 2008 bear market. From the top of the markets in October 2007 to March 2009, the S&P 500 Index fell 54% while the EAFE Index declined by 59%. An investor derived no added benefit from international stocks. This is especially critical in poor performing periods, where the movements between the primary U.S. stock index (S&P 500) and the EAFE is remarkably close. Table 2.3 lists the monthly correlations of the two major market indices. The correlation in the last bear market was 91% (see Table 2.3).

TABLE 2.3 Bear and Bull Market Correlation of Monthly Returns:
S&P 500 vs. EAFE

Bull Market: 1990–1999	0.54
Bear Market: 2000–2002	0.83
Bull Market: 2003–2007	0.65
Bear Market: 2007–2009	0.91
Correlation: 2000–2009	0.82

Source: Ibbottson.

In the most recent academic study[6] on the subject, "Uncorrelated: Assets Are Now Correlated", Richard Bernstein and Kari Pinkernell (2007) wrote that their analysis demonstrated that previously uncorrelated asset classes are now often highly correlated to the S&P 500, and their diversification benefits seem to be greatly reduced, if not completely eliminated. They wrote "investors should realize that these assets' risk-reduction benefits have largely vanished." The team examined 11 asset classes ranging from U.S. stocks to international stocks, hedge funds, and gold. They noted the increase in correlation among asset classes and the damage such an increase does to the benefits of diversification. They asserted further that "asset classes that were uncorrelated with the S&P 500 six years ago are now highly correlated." This included the Russell 2000 small-cap index, which maintained a correlation of .81 over the millennium decade.

This rise of correlation is due to many factors. Companies must now compete globally, not just domestically. Trade barriers have been dramatically reduced over the past 15 years. This has allowed companies to cross borders with a competitively priced product. The composition of the global stock indexes like the EAFE has also changed. The EAFE is now dominated by large global companies that compete within similar industries. There are other factors as well. There is considerable progress being made towards the alignment of regulations and corporate governance across the world. Areas under consolidation include accounting standards, treatment of minority shareholders, mergers and acquisitions, and shareholder value. As one illustration, the European Commission proposed all companies adopt International Accounting Standards in 2005, and Japan is moving in the same general direction today. In addition, data from major exchanges indicate that foreign ownership of stocks, while still relatively modest, is rising quickly.

Foreign owners hold about 25% of the stocks traded on the Tokyo Stock Exchange and about 15% of U.S.-traded stocks. In Europe, companies are increasingly purchasing stocks across the 12 countries of the European Union rather than in just their own. Finally, in recent years, investment managers and brokerage firms have been structuring their research activities globally, so that the same group of analysts follows a given industry across all markets. This has helped to increase the similarities in stock behavior across borders.

Many large U.S. companies count two-thirds or more of their revenues from outside the U.S. Coca-Cola, McDonald's, Texaco, and Texas Instruments are all companies that generate more than half of their revenue outside the U.S. Many U.S.-based and foreign companies have nearly identical revenue streams. For example, ExxonMobil, the largest member of the S&P 500 Index maintains 70% of its revenue abroad. United Kingdom–based British Petroleum, the biggest stock in the Morgan Stanley international index, has the same breakdown, with 30% of revenue derived from the U.S. The home country of the firm is no longer as relevant as the global economy continues to expand.

In addition, the barriers between the stock markets will most likely continue to drop. With the stock exchange mergers of 2011 between the London Stock Exchange and the parent company of the Toronto Stock Exchange, the Singapore Exchange and Australia's ASX, and the mammoth New York Stock Exchange with another to-be-determined solicitor, the world will soon have fewer exchanges. A 24-hour global exchange is a possibility within the next decade. This will only ensure that high correlations are here to stay. Increased correlation does not mean you should avoid international stocks. You may prefer to buy Total over ExxonMobil. You should simply not buy Exxon-Mobil just to maintain a home country bias. So considering the rising correlations of the traditional asset alternatives such as the EAFE and Russell 2000, can sector investing contribute to more diversified portfolios? Absolutely. Let's start with examining the differences in correlation between the major sectors alongside the S&P 500.

Table 2.4 shows return correlations for the market as measured by the S&P 500 and the 10 Morningstar sectors for the past decade.

Whereas the correlations over the preceding decade for the EAFE and the Russell 2000 are very high, several of the sectors within the S&P 500 have much lower relationships. Four sectors—utilities, health care, energy, and consumer staples—all

TABLE 2.4 Correlations for the Market

	S&P	CD	CS	E	F	H	I	M	T	U
S&P 500										
Consumer Discretionary	0.88									
Consumer Staples	0.56	0.69								
Energy	0.55	0.50	0.40							
Financials	0.82	0.75	0.68	0.42						
Health Care	0.59	0.47	0.66	0.38	0.55					
Industrials	0.90	0.85	0.58	0.61	0.80	0.58				
Materials	0.72	0.75	0.61	0.68	0.68	0.49	0.83			
Technology	0.82	0.76	0.31	0.42	0.48	0.40	0.70	0.55		
Utilities	0.41	0.47	0.47	0.61	0.47	0.51	0.52	0.47	0.58	

Source: Morningstar Sectors, based on monthly correlations, 1/2000 to 1/2010.

TABLE 2.5 Sector Return Matrix

	Best Performing	Return	Worst Performing	Return	Difference
1999	Technology	66.7%	Consumer Staples	−14.5%	81.2%
2000	Energy	24.9%	Technology	−42.0%	66.9%
2001	Health Care	0.4%	Technology	−22.8%	23.2%
2002	Health Care	−1.4%	Technology	−38.4%	36.9%
2003	Technology	39.5%	Consumer Staples	11.3%	28.2%
2004	Energy	33.9%	Health Care	1.7%	32.2%
2005	Energy	40.4%	Consumer Discretionary	−6.4%	46.8%
2006	Utilities	21.0%	Health Care	7.3%	13.6%
2007	Energy	36.7%	Financials	−18.6%	55.3%
2008	Consumer Staples	−15.0%	Financials	−55.3%	40.3%
2009	Technology	50.9%	Consumer Staples	14.2%	39.5%
2010	Industrials	27.8%	Health Care	3.3%	24.5%

Source: Morningstar, 1/1999 to 1/2010.

maintain correlations of less than 0.6 to the S&P 500 Index. Within the sectors, cross-correlations are distinctively temperate, with technology and staples maintaining a minuscule 0.31 correlation. Health care and energy maintain only a 0.38 correlation. By examining the divergent sector returns for the preceding decade, an investor can realize why cross-correlations for many sectors are so wide (see Table 2.5).

The wide disparity in sector returns validates the notion that sectors are just as important, if not more so, than international or cap size exposure.

Sector Volatility

Another critical factor is the inherent volatility of each major sector. We can measure this volatility through a statistic called beta. Back in the 1970s, researchers developed a statistic called beta to measure how the investment return of any asset moved vis-à-vis the overall market. While there are several ways to calculate beta, the most common method is to compare a stock's monthly returns to the S&P 500 Index's returns over the previous time period. With the beta of the S&P 500 Index set at 1.0, stocks that have tended to swing more than the market have betas above 1.0, whereas stocks that have fluctuated less than the market have betas below 1.0. All things being equal, a portfolio of stocks with betas averaging 0.80 would tend to rise 8% in a period when the S&P 500 rose 10%. The early high priests of modern portfolio theory argued that betas completely defined a stock's systematic risk (i.e., that portion of stock risk that cannot be eliminated by building a well-diversified portfolio of many stocks). Therefore, a diversified portfolio's expected return relative to the overall market should be proportional to that portfolio's beta. In theory, an investor who held a low-beta portfolio could expect to experience less risk than the market, but the cost would be a lower long-term return than market averages—there is no free lunch.

Well, it did not take long for investors to realize that beta did not work as advertised. The measure did a decent job of forecasting the expected risk levels of diversified portfolios, but not their expected returns. The tendency for high-beta portfolios to deliver weak long-term returns with well above average risk is well documented. To illustrate, in an April 2007 research paper entitled "The Volatility Effect: Lower Risk without Lower Return", David Blitz and Pim van Vliet[7] examined the relationship between long-term historical return volatility and risk-adjusted return for stocks worldwide. Ranking stocks based on historical volatility is closely similar to ranking them based on beta. Using monthly price and fundamental data for a large number of large-capitalization stocks over the period December 1985 through January 2006, the authors found the relationship between historical volatility and subsequent raw return is weak.

On a risk-adjusted basis, the least volatile tenth of stocks world-wide outperformed the most volatile tenth by an average 12% annually during 1986–2006. The outperformance of low-volatility stocks relative to high-volatility stocks in the European and Japanese stock markets is also of a comparable magnitude. Low-volatility stocks generally underperform (outperform) the market during up (down) months, with the underperformance during up months being considerably smaller than the outperformance during down months. High-volatility stocks exhibit the opposite behavior. The volatility effect is also robust across subperiods and for different intervals of historical volatility. In summary, investors overpay for volatile stocks over the long haul, most dramatically during bear markets.

Additional studies have confirmed the low-beta effect. Ric Thomas and Robert Shapiro of State Street Global Advisors published a paper[8] testing low-beta portfolios versus high-beta ones. In their research, the authors simulated portfolios filled with stocks from the Russell 3000 Index that were broken into deciles based on volatility factors. Low-volatility portfolios not only exhibited less risk than the overall market over a 20-year span, but they also outperformed portfolios built with higher-volatility stocks. The findings are consistent with findings showing that the commonly held investment theory that you can do no better than the market without taking on more risk is flawed.

About 70% of all stocks have betas between 0.5 and 2.0. Most stocks' betas are fairly consistent through time as long as the underlying companies do not evolve too quickly. Therefore, a stock with an extremely low or high beta will generally moderate back toward more typical beta values over time. Stock betas tend to be uncorrelated to most commonly used stock-selection criteria, with two major exceptions: Low-beta stocks tend to have above-average dividend yields and below-average earnings growth forecasts. This means that if you employ strategies that emphasize strong fundamentals, cheap equity valuation, or

TABLE 2.6 Sector Beta Matrix

	Median Beta	Percentage of Stocks with Beta Less than 1
Consumer Discretionary	1.27	30%
Consumer Staples	0.82	68%
Energy	0.98	52%
Financials	0.95	55%
Health Care	0.81	56%
Industrials	1.27	33%
Technology	1.59	19%
Materials	1.30	32%
Utilities	0.67	82%

Source: Charles Schwab Center for Financial Research, Largest 3200 Stocks, 2008.

high momentum, you can find stocks to your liking that also have below-average betas. With a little more research, you can also find low-beta stocks with nice earnings growth rates. But remember, low-beta investing will tend to put the very fastest-growing or most speculative stocks off-limits—not a bad compromise. Listed in Table 2.6 are the average betas for all of the major sectors.

It clearly appears that certain sectors have maintained a lower beta than others, including consumer staples, health care, and utilities. Energy surprisingly also had a beta less than 1 over the preceding 10 years. This is most likely due to the wide assortment of dividend-paying blue chips within the sector, such as ExxonMobil, Chevron, and ConocoPhilips. Sector weight changes are also a critical factor an investor must pay attention to. These alterations can occur quickly over time. As sectors go in and out of favor over time, overvaluation becomes very probable. The best example in the past 20 years is in the technology sector. The technology sector grew from 8% of the S&P 500 in 1994 to nearly 30% by March of 2000, as the Internet mania took

TABLE 2.7 Sector Weights since 1994, S&P 500

	1994	1999	2004	2009
Consumer Discretionary	14.9%	12.7%	11.9%	9.4%
Consumer Staples	13.2%	7.2%	10.5%	13.0%
Energy	10.0%	5.6%	7.2%	12.0%
Financials	10.7%	13.0%	20.6%	13.3%
Health Care	9.2%	9.3%	12.7%	13.5%
Industrials	13.0%	9.9%	11.8%	9.7%
Technology	8.6%	29.2%	16.1%	18.8%
Materials	7.1%	3.0%	3.1%	3.1%
Utilities	4.8%	2.2%	2.9%	3.9%

Source: Morningstar,1/1994 to 1/2010.

hold in the late 1990s. After the collapse of the sector, the weighting of the technology fell dramatically to 16% by 2004. Financial stocks also had a spectacular climb, starting at a weight of only 10% in 1994. The sector slowly climbed over the next decade until it made up nearly 30% of the overall index by 2007. If you have money in an index fund, you are riding this sector overconcentration up and down in economic and market cycles. This can expose investors to an undue amount of risk, especially if the sector in question has experienced a tremendous amount of momentum and is highly overvalued. Table 2.7 shows the historical sector weights from 1994.

An astute investor will examine these sector trends and minimize exposure to sectors that have risen above their historical weight.

Major Sectors

There are nine major sectors of the economy, which are

- Basic materials
- Consumer discretionary

- Consumer staples
- Energy
- Financial
- Health care
- Industrial
- Technology
- Utilities

A basic description of each major sector follows.

Basic Materials: Chemicals, Metals and Mining, Steel

Most of the companies in this category produce commodities whose sale price tends to converge with the cost of production, especially in the low-inflation environment as we have seen in recent years. These companies generally maintain high debt levels and poor long-term growth characteristics. The sector can perform well during periods of high inflation.

Consumer Discretionary: Autos, Building and Construction, Publishing, Retail

As with capital goods, these stocks perform poorly heading into economic slowdowns and perform well in expanding economies. This sector is less sensitive to overall interest rates (consumers buy homes, cars, and furnishings very happily on credit while corporate purchasers worry about budgets).

Consumer Staples: Beverages, Food, Tobacco

This sector is traditionally recession-proof (consumers buy toothpaste and beer no matter what the state of the economy). The consumer group companies are attractive as their overall volatility is low and the prospects for future growth are strong. The sector is a solid defensive investment during poor economic times.

Energy: Oil and Gas, Drillers

The energy sector has a different dynamic than the basic materials group because of regulation by the OPEC cartel. The energy sector has been one of the most compelling sectors over the past 20 years as oil prices have climbed from $15 a barrel in the 1990s. Many energy stocks are also attractive for their higher than average dividend yields.

Industrial: Aerospace/Defense, Electrical Machinery

The industrial sector consists basically of the "old economy" stocks. This group is in its mature stage; with limited prospects for future growth. Although this sector can have exceptional investment returns in economic recoveries, overall performance is expected to be subpar.

Health Care: Pharmaceuticals, Medical Devices, Biotechnology, Managed Care

Companies in this sector also are relatively recession-proof; when you need medicine, you need medicine. Conventional pharmaceutical companies offer relatively predictable returns. Biotech companies offer outsize returns with higher risks. Hospitals, HMOs, and other care facilities offer further diversification within the sector.

Financials: Major Banks, Insurance, Brokerages

Stock prices in this sector used to be tightly correlated with changes in interest rates. In recent years, the companies have become more adept at managing interest-rate risk, but the stock prices still tend to move higher when rates move lower. Consolidation and cost control have been much bigger drivers of financial stock prices in recent years. Banks and finance companies tend to do poorly heading into recessions: bad loans increase and transaction income dries up. Insurance companies, particularly property and casualty companies, suffer when underwriting competition drives down premiums.

Technology: Semiconductors, Internet, Software

Growth in this sector is subject to the same pressures as other capital goods. Even when overall demand is high, companies are at great risk from "paradigm shifts" (e.g., mainframe computers supplanted by desktop computers). The sector is considered the most volatile of all areas of the economy.

Utilities: Electricity, Water, Gas

Utilities are companies that purchase and redistribute resources such as electricity, water, and gas. This includes companies that are responsible for power generation and infrastructure maintenance. This sector also performs well during recessions and period of low growth. Stocks within the sector are considered defensive in nature and also carry higher than average dividend yields.

Utilizing Sectors in Market Cycles

Financial markets endeavor to predict the state of the economy, anywhere from three to six months into the future. That means the market cycle is usually well ahead of the economic cycle. This is crucial to remember, because as the economy is in the pits of a recession, the market begins to look ahead to a recovery. The following sections describe the four basic stages of the economic cycle along with some associated telltale signs Again, keep in mind that these usually trail the market cycle by a few months.

Late Recession

The economy has been retracting, quarter-over-quarter; interest rates are being reduced by the Federal Reserve Bank; consumer expectations have bottomed; and the yield curve is steepening. Sectors that have historically performed the best during this stage include

- Basic materials
- Technology
- Industrials

Early Recovery

This occurs when the economy has started to advance off the bottom. Spending by consumers is now rising, industrial production is growing, and the yield curve has officially turned upward sloping. Historically, successful sectors at this juncture include

- Industrials (near the beginning)
- Technology (near the beginning)
- Consumer discretionary
- Energy (near the end)

Late Recovery

In this stage, the Federal Reserve Bank is raising interest rates, and the yield curve is flattening. Consumer expectations are beginning to decline, and industrial production is flat or declining. Historically profitable sectors in this stage include

- Energy (near the beginning)
- Consumer staples (near the end)
- Health care (near the end)

Early Recession

This is where the economy is suffering from waning GDP growth. Consumer expectations are in the pits, industrial production is declining, interest rates are high and peaking, and the yield curve is inverted or flat. Historically, the following sectors have found favor during these difficult times

- Health care
- Consumer staples
- Utilities

Can a sector rotation strategy based on economic cycles work? Using 33 years of data, professors C. Mitchell Conover and Gerald Jensen found that a sector rotation strategy can earn consistent excess returns while requiring only infrequent rebalancing.[9] The winning strategy placed greater emphasis on cyclical stocks during periods of Federal Reserve Bank easing and involved overweighting defensive stocks during periods of Federal Reserve Bank tightening. Interestingly, the benefits from the rotation strategy accrue predominantly during periods of poor equity market performance, which is when performance enhancement is most valued by investors. The authors found that a sector rotation portfolio that maintained equal weights among the six cyclical sectors during periods of expansive monetary policy significantly outperforms a market portfolio by an average 3.78% per year. Since large directional monetary policy changes by the Federal Reserve are infrequent, investors can easily follow trends in monetary policy to make alterations in their portfolios.

Sector Performance

Utilizing a sector strategy should have some merit at this point. I have demonstrated that sectors provide more diversification than typically selected assets. Which sectors have performed the best over an extended period of cycles? In March 2005, Dr. Jeremy J. Siegel published a book titled *The Future for Investors: Why the Tried and the True Triumph Over the Bold and the New*. In the publication, Dr. Siegel found five sectors that have outperformed the S&P 500 during a period from 1957 to 2003. These five sectors were health care, consumer staples, energy, technology, and financials. This data is also confirmed through an examination of sector returns from the inception of sector funds in the mid-1980s. Since 1986, I have tracked the sector fund return data through Lipper and the SPDR funds (see Figure 2.1).

The second chart listed below indicates performance for each sector from 1986 through 2010. In my own study, the Consumer Staples sector maintained the largest performance edge of

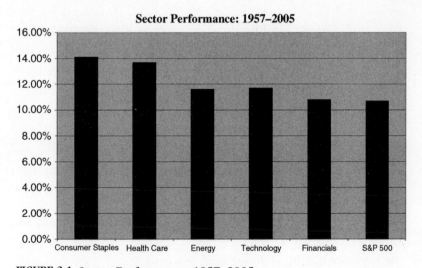

FIGURE 2.1 Sector Performance: 1957–2005
Source: "Long-Term Returns on the Original S&P 500 Companies." Jeremy J. Siegel, *Financial Analysts Journal* (Jan/Feb 2006).

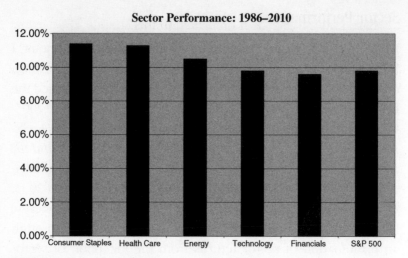

FIGURE 2.2 Sector Performance: 1986–2010

Source: Lipper Inc, A Reuters Company, January 1, 1986 through December 31, 1998. Annualized Returns. Financials measured by Financial Services Funds, health care by Healthcare/Biotechnology funds, consumer staples by Fidelity Consumer Staples Fund, energy by Natural Resources Funds, and technology by Science and Technology Funds. Returns from January 1, 1999 through December 31, 2010 are measured by SPDR sector ETF funds.

any sector. Health care was a close second, followed by the energy, financials, and technology sectors. You may note that the top two performers, health care and consumer staples, are both considered defensive sectors. These sectors also maintain a low beta, which confirms the "low-beta effect" presented earlier. See Figure 2.2.

Energy stocks had the best performance of any cyclical sector, and they also provide an excellent hedge against inflation. Inflation has an adverse impact on the stock market. In the last two periods of high inflation (1974, 1979), stocks performed very poorly. If investors are to consider sectors as a primary component to their investment strategy, three criteria should be used:

- Superior historical investment returns
- Low correlations with other sectors
- Low volatility or beta

Based on the evidence presented in this chapter, the sectors that meet all of these criteria are the health care, consumer staples, and energy sectors. These three sectors have offered investors superior returns, a predominate amount of low-beta candidates, and low cross-correlations with other major sectors. Two other sectors are also worthy of mention and attention: financials and technology. Both sectors have outperformed the market indices in Jeremy J. Siegel's study, and also offer some compelling cross-correlation statistics. Unfortunately, these sectors had been fraught with higher risk over the previous decade. A prudent investor will examine these sectors in detail for added diversification purposes; however, any investor should be cognizant of the higher risks that are associated with these sectors.

CHAPTER 3

The Health Care Sector

*Be careful about reading health books, you may
die of a misprint.*

Mark Twain

The U.S. health care industry is the largest single slice of the
U.S. economy, amounting to expenditures of $2.6 trillion in
2010. The health care sector is quite diverse and includes pharmaceutical companies, health care facilities, managed care/
HMOs, medical supply manufacturers, and biotechnology. Each
of these subsectors is affected by different issues, but all share a
common goal: to profit while preserving or restoring the health
of their clients.

This sector represents 11.0% of the market capitalization of
the S&P 500, making it the fifth largest sector. The health care sector has delivered exceptional investment returns over the 24-year
period ending December 31, 2010. As demonstrated in Chapter 2,
the category's returns were the second-highest of any sector; an
11.3% annualized return. Just as important are the defensive characteristics. Since 1986, the health care sector has suffered only five
losing years (see Table 2.1). This is the lowest number of negative
return years of any of the major sectors within the S&P 500 stock
index. The sector also fared well in 1990, 1994, and 2000, losing
years in the general market. Health care stocks generally

TABLE 3.1 Health Care Sector: Losing Years since 1986

1987	−1.16%
1992	−6.65%
2001	−12.55%
2002	−18.85%
2008	−23.43%

Source: Lipper Inc; A Reuters Company, January 1, 1986 through December 31, 1998. Annualized Returns. Financials measured by Financial Services Funds, health care by Healthcare/Biotechnology funds, consumer staples by Fidelity Consumer Staples Fund, energy by Natural Resources Funds, and technology by Science and Technology Funds. Returns from January 1, 1999 through December 31, 2010 are measured by SPDR sector ETF funds.

outperform the market when the economy is heading into recession and many other stocks are losing value (see Table 3.1).

Reasons to Own a Health Care Firm

There are four primary characteristics that make owning a health care firm attractive:

- Aging of the global population base
- Advances in medical technology will continue to accelerate
- Growth in emerging market incomes
- Stable investment returns despite economic cycles

The grouping of these factors should enable health care stocks to generate the earnings that make these holdings attractive for long-term investors. One caveat is the regulatory environment, which can have a sizeable impact on how health care firms operate.

Demographics

One of the major supports of the health care sector is the graying of America—and the world. It renders health care a true long-term growth story. The world's population is simply getting older, and this will lead to increased demand for and greater spending on health care solutions. Growth will also be boosted as standards and expectations rise, generating demand for better equipment, technologies, and procedures. Health care economics will be dramatically shaped by the march of the baby boom generation toward retirement age. According to data from the U.S. Administration on Aging, people aged 65 years and older consume four times as much health care per capita as people under 65. When Medicaid and Medicare programs were enacted in the 1960s, the 65+ age group constituted 10% of the total population. This number has grown to 12.8% of the total in 2010. Despite this relatively modest increase, health care expenditures soared during this time frame due to technological increases that led to new drugs and procedures.

In coming years, we face an acceleration of growth in the ranks of the elderly. By 2020, the population of the 65+ group is estimated to grow from 40 million today to 53.3 million. Therefore, the 65+ group will grow to 16.3% of the total U.S. population in 2020. The Labor Department's outlook projects that the labor force will continue to age along with the baby boomers through 2014. The number of workers in the 55 and older group is expected to increase 4.1% annually, more than four times faster than the overall labor force, which should increase 1% per year, the same as the growth in the working age population, and represents a considerable slowing from previous decades. The labor force participation rate of workers older than 55 has been increasing since the mid-1980s and is projected to continue increasing at least to 2014. Older workers are living longer, so they have to work longer to support themselves and to have health care benefits. The demand for health care, which currently accounts for a record 21% of consumer spending on goods and services, will continue to boom throughout the next several decades. According to a new study released from economists at the Center for Medicare and Medicaid Services (CMS) spending on health care should nearly double over the next decade, reaching $4.3 trillion in 2017. This will represent an astounding 19.5% of U.S. GDP, or nearly one-fifth of the U.S. economy. The study's authors expect spending to grow at a steady annual rate of 6.7% over the next 10 years, continuing to outpace inflation and economic growth.

Advances in Medical Technology

For nearly all of the past four decades, spending on health care in the United States grew more rapidly than the economy. As a result, the share of national income devoted to health care nearly tripled. This ongoing spending growth pervaded all parts of the health system, including the nation's public insurance programs. Although many factors contributed to that growth, most analysts have concluded that a substantial portion of the long-term rise resulted from the health care system's use of new medical services that were made possible by technological advances, or what some analysts term the "increased capabilities of medicine." Major advances in medical science have allowed health care providers to diagnose and treat illness in ways that were previously impossible.

Technological innovation can theoretically reduce costs and, for many types of goods and services, it often does. Historically, however, the nature of technological advances in medicine and the changes in clinical practice that followed them have tended to raise overall spending and result in higher earnings for medical firms. Technological advances are likely to yield new, desirable medical services in the future, fueling further spending growth and imposing difficult choices between spending on health care and spending on other priorities. If the health care system adopts new services rapidly and applies them broadly in the future—as it has tended to do in the past—large increases in health care spending are likely to continue.

Rising Incomes in Emerging Markets

As societies grow and become wealthier, one primary discretionary purchase item that becomes more common is spending on health care. We can measure how health care becomes more widespread within societies through what is known as income elasticity. This measures what percentage of income, if increased, would be further spent on a certain category. According to a paper published by Christine Borger, Thomas Rutherford, and Gregory Won, income elasticity for health care estimates to between 0 and 1.6. In the paper titled "Forecasting the Cost of U.S. Healthcare," Robert Fogel[1] of the University of Chicago claimed that income elasticity for medical care amounted to 1.6 (i.e., a society will use 16% on health care when incomes goes up by 10%). Fogel claimed that expenditures on health care are driven primarily by demand for new services, which are stimulated by higher incomes as well as advances in health care technology that make health interventions increasingly effective but also expensive.

Spending on pharmaceutical products has been shown to be directly correlated to higher incomes (Figure 3.1). The Torreya Partners group calculated the relationship between incomes and spending on pharmaceutical products, as shown in the figure. The highest-income countries (U.S., Canada, Norway, Australia) also spend a much higher amount on health care than lower-income countries (Mexico, Poland, Hungary).

The developed world has provided for the bulk of total health care spending over the preceding half century. As the elasticity of demand for health care is positively correlated to higher income levels, countries such as Brazil, China, and India represent a high resource of future health care spending.

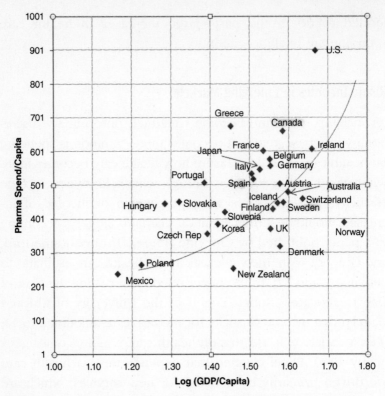

FIGURE 3.1 Pharma Spending Is Higher in Higher-Income Countries
Source: OECD Health Data; Torreya Partners calculations.

Economic Factors

Health care sector stocks are generally noncyclical (or at any rate, less cyclical) because the demand for health care products and drugs does not depend on the state of the economy. Over the past 10 years, the health care sector has enjoyed stable investment returns despite the economic environment. Economic forecasts for moderate growth and declining interest rates are advantageous for the health care industry in general. When growth is moderate and money is tight, consumers may put off buying new cars and computers, but they will nevertheless continue to pay for medicines and health services. The sector tends to do best when the economy is sluggish or in recession.

Additional Factors

Outside of the United States, most health care expenditures have come under nearly complete government control. The United States has the lone remaining predominantly private health care system among developed countries. However, the largest single payer in our system is the federal government; through its Medicare and Medicaid programs. As a result, health care economics are increasingly governed by public policy, which is influenced by societal opinion, budgetary constraint, and tax policy. Demographic, social, and political trends are likely to increase government's role as a payer of health care costs. As costs increase and the population ages, the government will take on a larger role in the health care sector. Changes in government reimbursement, taxation, research rules, or FDA drug application processing make it more or less economically appealing to invest in new health care products, drugs, new drug research, and so forth. Future problems ranging from recent presidential efforts to revamp the entire health system, to federal and state laws that alter reimbursement rules, to slow approval of new drugs by the Food and Drug Administration could all have a dramatic impact on the health care sector.

Sub-Sector Analysis

THE PHARMACEUTICAL INDUSTRY The pharmaceutical industry comprises over 60% of the health care sector and 5% of the benchmark S&P 500 Index. Pharmaceutical companies sell products necessary for health, not for some discretionary need. These products usually represent a must-repeat purchase, no matter the economic situation. Pharmaceutical companies are among the best-known firms operating within the health care sector. They include giants like Pfizer and Merck, which make drugs such as Lipitor and Gardisal. One of the major challenges facing pharmaceutical firms is increased competition from generic drug manufacturers. The Food and Drug

Administration (FDA) has estimated that over the next five years, 858 drugs will lose patent protection, opening the doors to generic competition. Generic drug manufacturers are growing increasingly sophisticated in their ability to produce generic versions of a medication as soon as it loses patent protection. Large pharmaceutical companies, which have viewed generic producers as their sworn enemies, are now wondering whether it would be a successful strategy to get into the generic market. Some firms, such as Novartis, have recently made acquisitions into the generic field. Other issues that have surfaced during the past decade are safety related. Given the recent problems with Cox-2 drugs such as Vioxx, the FDA is under increased scrutiny to ensure the safety of new drugs.

Once powerful profit machines, big pharmaceutical firms are stumbling up against dry product pipelines, fierce competition from generic manufacturers, consumer concerns about safety and false marketing claims, and the threat of a larger government role in drug purchases and pricing. While health care reform has dominated headlines, drug companies have come through the debate relatively untouched. Early in the health care reform negotiations of 2010, the drug industry promised the Obama administration it would contribute $80 billion in savings to help finance proposed reform over the next ten years. In return, the industry's basic pricing structure would remain intact under the reform proposals being considered by legislators in Washington. The tradeoff for the industry is that the expansion of coverage to more than 40 million uninsured would give pharmaceutical firms a larger customer base. The revenue growth would translate to pure profit, because the cost of creating a medication is not in the production of the pill itself, but the research that goes into discovering a new therapy.

Pharmaceutical companies' high margins are dependent on exclusive rights to market the products of their costly research efforts. Patent protection usually guarantees high margins on new drugs for at least a decade. When patents expire, generic drug manufacturers erode pharmaceutical companies' profits by selling comparable drugs at discounts of 80 to 90%. To move into new areas of growth, pharmaceutical companies are acquiring or partnering with biotech companies that make more sophisticated products. Biotech medications, which must typically be delivered by infusion in a physician's office, tend to be more expensive and highly targeted to patients compared with the traditional chemical-based compounds that the pharmaceutical industry usually manufactures.

Pharmaceutical companies have also realized that they need to expand outside their niche markets. Most companies have diversified or have made plans to diversify into different areas mainly in the developing world, in order to boost revenues. Countries that IMS Health has cited as emerging countries include India, China, Brazil, Turkey, Russia, South Korea, and Mexico. As mentioned earlier in this chapter, new profits will be generated from emerging economies in the future. Moreover, over half a billion people will ultimately be able to afford Western medicines. With a projected growth of 13–14% in the emerging markets, and pharmaceutical stocks at low historical valuations, the industry will most likely remain a high weight of the health care sector (see Table 3.2).

The Medical Device Industry

The medical device industry comprises 13.3% of the health care sector. Also known as the medical equipment and supply industry, it includes manufacturers and distributors of products and supplies used in health care delivery. These include surgical and medical instruments, orthopedic devices and surgical supplies, diagnostic reagents, electro-medical equipment, X-ray equipment, and dental equipment. Depending on the degree of technology elements in these products, they can be further grouped

TABLE 3.2 Major Pharmaceutical Firms

	Industry	Market Cap
Johnson & Johnson	Drug Manufacturers, Major	181,984.51
Novartis AG	Drug Manufacturers, Major	169,789.33
Pfizer, Inc.	Drug Manufacturers, Major	166,160.77
Roche Holding AG	Drug Manufacturers, Major	147,187.70
Merck & Co, Inc	Drug Manufacturers, Major	115,376.54
GlaxoSmithKline PLC	Drug Manufacturers, Major	112,644.99
Sanofi Aventis ADR	Drug Manufacturers, Major	102,384.98
Abbott Laboratories	Drug Manufacturers, Major	83,029.80
Novo Nordisk A/S	Drug Manufacturers, Major	75,300.00
AstraZeneca PLC	Drug Manufacturers, Major	71,975.37
Bayer AG	Drug Manufacturers, Major	68,611.86
Bristol-Myers Squibb Company	Drug Manufacturers, Major	48,791.27
Eli Lilly and Company	Drug Manufacturers, Major	44,813.27
Allergan, Inc.	Drug Manufacturers, Major	25,449.36

Source: Standard & Poors.

into two distinct sub-sectors: conventional hospital supplies and medical technology products.

Conventional hospital supplies account for 40% of the industry's total worldwide sales. This market is dominated by a relatively small number of large manufacturers, including Cardinal Health, McKesson, and AmerisourceBergen. Medical technology products control a relatively small share of the market and serve a specialized patient population but have much higher profit margins. The two-tier industry is dominated by a few leading manufacturers such as Boston Scientific, Baxter International, Medtronic, and Becton Dickinson, which offer a comprehensive line of both conventional hospital supplies and technology products to a broad market segment. A larger number of companies in this industry are small and medium-sized firms that produce limited lines of specialty medical devices and products.

The medical device industry is highly regulated, and the regulatory environment at home and abroad has serious implications for industry performance. Domestically, medical device firms devote considerable resources toward product approval processes, clinical trials, user fees, and plant audits. The U.S. FDA is conscious of the need to streamline regulatory processes and procedures and is proactively trying to address the concerns of U.S. firms. Issues related to reimbursement rates for medical devices are a primary concern for U.S. medical device companies, as an adequate reimbursement rate usually determines whether a product will be viable in a given market. In the United States, there are several players involved in establishing reimbursement rates. The Department of Health and Human Services' Center for Medical and Medicaid Services (HHS/CMS) is the central agent of control and change in the area of cost containment and reimbursement for Medicare and Medicaid. Other players in the U.S. market include HMOs, private health insurance companies, and the Veterans' Administration.

The U.S. market represents such a large percentage of the global market that a low reimbursement rate in the U.S. market may make a product uneconomical to produce globally. Reimbursement rates are considered so important that firms are advised to start working with CMS as early as possible in the product approval process. Notably, many medical device firms in the U.S. apply for and receive the CE mark (the regulatory approval process used in the European Union) before seeking FDA approval, or work on certifying their products in both systems concurrently. The new health care law will also bring a raft of changes to the medical device industry, including an excise tax on many medical devices, and the tax is causing a lot of consternation in one of Minnesota's most prominent industries. The medical device excise tax aims to raise $20 billion over 10 years when it goes into effect in 2013. See Table 3.3.

TABLE 3.3 Major Medical Device and Distribution Firms

	Industry	Market Cap
Medtronic, Inc.	Medical Devices	45,790.72
Baxter International, Inc.	Medical Devices	34,348.14
Covidien, Ltd.	Medical Devices	28,494.76
Thermo Fisher Scientific, Inc.	Medical Devices	25,057.48
Stryker Corporation	Medical Devices	24,832.28
McKesson, Inc.	Medical Devices	21,843.68
Becton Dickinson & Co.	Medical Devices	19,595.78
St Jude Medical, Inc.	Medical Devices	17,073.88
Cardinal Health, Inc.	Medical Devices	15,864.04
Intuitive Surgical, Inc.	Medical Devices	13,862.76
Zimmer Holdings, Inc.	Medical Devices	13,107.10
AmerisourceBergen Corporation	Medical Devices	11,459.86

Source: Standard & Poor's.

The Biotechnology Industry

The biotechnology industry has a history of less than three decades. It is different from the traditional pharmaceutical industry primarily in the technology employed. Most traditional pharmaceutical drugs are relatively simple molecules that have been found primarily through trial and error to treat the symptoms of a disease or illness. Biotechnology pharmaceuticals are outsized biological molecules identified as proteins, and these usually target the essential mechanisms and pathways of a malady. Biotechnology involves using recombinant DNA technology to manipulate living organisms or biological components at cellular, sub-cellular, or molecular levels to create marketable products for human or animal health needs. The rapid advance in biomedical and molecular cellular biology research has ushered in a new wave of biotechnology. The combination of genome research and information technology has created an exciting new technology frontier—bioinformatics—which promises a revolution in the way diseases will be treated. As more and more traditional pharmaceutical companies are engaged in biological drug discovery, the line between the pharmaceutical and bio-technology firms is becoming less clear.

Biotech companies are now operating in a new normal, where access to capital is more difficult than ever. In general, venture capitalists are being more selective and are reserving funds for existing portfolio investments. Some funding is being directed to finance R&D assets or projects, with potentially faster returns, instead of starting new companies. IPO investors are primarily seeking more mature, de-risked investments, and IPOs are pricing below companies' expectations. Other public funding is increasingly concentrated in a smaller number of compa-nies. Big pharmaceutical companies still need to acquire promising products for their pipelines, but recent mega-mergers and efforts to exit therapeutic categories have reduced the num-ber of potential buyers for any given biotech asset. The global biotechnology market generated $98 billion in 2010 sales, dem-onstrating a year-on-year growth of 10.7%. The period from 2005 to 2010 was a lucrative period for the biotechnology mar-ket, as it increased earnings at an annual rate of over 12%. Large firms in this arena include Amgen, Celgene, Gilead Sciences, and Biogen IDEC (see Table 3.4).

TABLE 3.4 Major Biotechnology Firms

	Industry	Market Cap
Amgen, Inc.	Biotechnology	56,746.10
Gilead Sciences, Inc.	Biotechnology	31,627.78
Celgene Corp.	Biotechnology	28,168.41
Biogen Idec, Inc.	Biotechnology	23,370.67
Life Technologies Corp	Biotechnology	9,757.04

Source: Standard & Poor's.

The Health Care Providers Industry

The major players in the health care providers industry include United Healthcare, Aetna, Cigna, and Wellpoint. The health care providers industry is composed of a continuum of plans exercising various degrees of cost and control. Listed from least to most controlled are managed indemnity plans, preferred provider organizations (PPO), point-of-service (POS) plans, and health maintenance organizations (HMO).

Apart from deriving revenue from insurance premiums, health insurance companies also draw revenue from investments, though only a small fraction of industry income is related to investment activity. The U.S. population is aging, which is an important indicator of demand for health insurance coverage in the long run. Older individuals are more likely to use medical coverage than their younger, healthier counterparts. Consequently, the aging population is expected to support industry growth. Many of the major industry players, such as United Healthcare, made a number of acquisitions during the past five years and are expected to continue such activity over the ensuing decade. The industry is expected to continue to consolidate, as insurers try to cut costs and improve profitability. At the same time, larger firms benefit from greater bargaining power in determining health care rates with medical providers such as doctors, hospitals, and pharmacies.

As the Patient Protection and Affordable Care Act takes effect, notwithstanding recent congressional and judicial challenges, more issues driving uncertainty will likely arise requiring health care investors in the near future to do more reshuffling. Another primary focus of the health insurance industry will be the medical loss ratio compliance provisions of the Health Care Reform Act, which became effective in 2011. Carriers are required to maintain a minimum medical loss ratio (percent of insurance premium dollars allocated to providing care) of 80%

TABLE 3.5 Major Health Care Providers Firms

	Industry	Mkt Cap
Unitedhealth Group, Inc.	Health Care Provider	54,767.77
WellPoint, Inc.	Health Care Provider	30,026.56
Aetna, Inc.	Health Care Provider	17,419.05
Cigna Corp.	Health Care Provider	13,401.31
Humana	Health Care Provider	13,377.25

Source: Standard & Poor's.

for individual and small group policies and 85% for large commercial policies. As part of the Act, the sector will be affected by many aspects of health insurance reform including individual and employer mandates, a tax on high-cost health plans, an annual industry fee/tax of $6.7 billion, cost shifting from Medicare and Medicaid cuts, and critically, an increase in the number of covered lives (see Table 3.5).

The Health Care Facilities Industry

The health care facilities industry includes hospitals, acute care facilities, rehabilitation facilities, nursing homes, assisted living facilities, and home health care services. Major players in this sub-sector include Tenet, HCA, Health Management Associates, and ManorCare. Healthcare service providers have suffered almost two decades of increasingly restrictive reimbursement policies from both government and private insurers. Reductions in reimbursement for services have been particularly brutal during the past five years. Physicians have endured significant cuts in income, nursing home and home health care providers have been put in financial intensive care, and hospitals were plunged into increasing distress. Recently, the government has added back funding to this distressed industry, improving the fundamentals of the major players. As part of the Health Care Reform Act, the benefits of expanded health insurance coverage over

TABLE 3.6 Major Health Care Facilities Firms

	Industry	Market Cap
HCA Holdings	Health Care Facilities	17,762.12
Tenet Healthcare	Health Care Facilities	3,096.88

Source: Standard & Poor's.

time will outweigh the $155 billion hospitals and health systems will lose in lower Medicare and Medicaid payments. Hospitals and health systems could see revenue improvements in excess of $170 billion as a result of reductions in bad debt and increased utilization of services (see Table 3.6).

INVESTING IN THE HEALTH CARE SECTOR   The health care sector should represent a larger percentage of your overall portfolio than any other stock sector. This large weight reflects the fact that the sector provides an exceptional long-term investment return with terrific defensive characteristics. This sector will perform best during a recession and offset losses in the more economically sensitive sectors. Stock selection within the health care sector should concentrate on pharmaceuticals, with the balance of money in the four other sub-sectors listed previously. Investors should observe the following guidelines:

- Concentration should be in pharmaceuticals.
- Select companies of a large size (5 billion market cap >).
- Favor industry leaders within each sub-sector.
- Attempt to add to your portfolio sub-sectors that are out of favor (see Chapter 11).
- Add to health care investment when the economy is near the end of an economic boom. If the Federal Reserve starts raising interest rates, increase exposure to health care.

FIGURE 3.2 Case Study No. 1: Zimmer, July 2009
Source: Charts provided by Commodity Systems, Inc. (CSI), 2012.

The financial meltdown of 2008 had a dramatic impact on the share prices of all stocks, including those in the health care sector. Although the sector had a double-digit loss during the period, the loss was much less than that of the overall market. Zimmer's core operational activities include orthopedic device development, manufacturing, and marketing. The firm focused primarily on joint reconstruction, where it remains a key leader in knee and hip implants. Knee and hip implants accounted for 72% of the firm's sales in 2008. The balance was generated from several other orthopedic niches, including surgical tools, spine implants, and trauma devices. The stock had collapsed from a high of $91 a share in 2007 to the low $30s by the beginning of 2009. Although a prudent investor would generally cycle into other sectors coming out of a recession, I felt Zimmer had more in common with the consumer discretionary sector in regard to performance metrics. The benefit of Zimmer, however, was that the firm still was primarily a health care firm, benefiting from the long-term trends of increased capital spending within the sector.

(continued)

(continued)

I examined the fundamentals of Zimmer in detail, starting with my favorite ratios pulled from the balance sheet and income statement, including the information shown in Table 3.7.

TABLE 3.7 Ratios

2008 E.P.S.	$3.73
Current Ratio	1.12
Debt/Equity	15%
Interest Cover	8.2
Operating Margin	36.5%
Net Margin	20.5%
Price/Sales	0.8
FCF Yield	9.3%

Source: Standard & Poor's.

My conclusions are as follows:

- Zimmer was the industry leader in the knee and hip replacement industry, outpacing other firms in nearly every measure of efficiency, profitability, and growth rates.
- Zimmer actually increased its sales during a very difficult 2008. Debt ratios had declined in the previous three years even despite the firm's high capital costs.
- Zimmer had a very low valuation and an expected growth rate of 12% for the next five years. This compared very favorably with its low P/E ratio of 10.
- Zimmer had traded at a price/sales ratio range of 1.5 to 5.8. The current ratio was at the lowest end of the historical spread.
- Zimmer had a very low debt ratio and a strong interest coverage ratio. If the recession got worse during 2009, I felt Zimmer could weather the storm quite well.

- Over the past 12 months, Zimmer Holdings had generated $1,015.0 million in cash on net income of $717.2 million. That meant it turned 24.2% of its revenue into free cash flow, a superlative measure. At this level, Zimmer had a free cash flow yield of over 10%. This yield was much higher than our minimum 4% criterion at the time (AAA Corporate Bond Yield).

I felt that Zimmer presented an excellent long-term investment opportunity. Considering the price of Zimmer had fallen nearly 60% during the past year, I also felt the downside was limited due to the low historical P/S ratio and the company's strong financial wherewithal. If the economy rebounded during the next two years due to the fiscal stimulus plans promoted by President Obama, Zimmer with its discretionary income component would be one of the primary beneficiaries within the health care sector. I purchased shares in client accounts at $39 a share in July of that year.

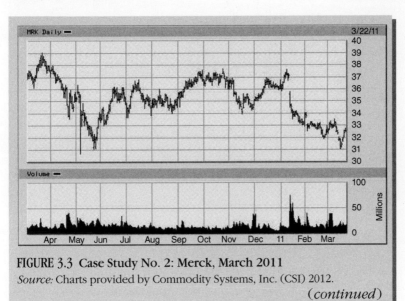

FIGURE 3.3 Case Study No. 2: Merck, March 2011
Source: Charts provided by Commodity Systems, Inc. (CSI) 2012.

(*continued*)

(*continued*)

Stocks in the pharmaceutical sub-sector were in the sick ward throughout most of the past decade. Over the previous few years, several large pharmaceutical companies such as Pfizer and Merck dramatically reduced earnings expectations. The AMEX pharmaceutical index had fallen from a high of $445 in 2001 to $295 by early 2011. Almost every pharmaceutical firm was out of favor with Wall Street. With health care being my top investment sector due to its extremely attractive profile of long-term return and future demographics, I was adding to the pharmaceutical sector throughout the past 18 months.

My top target for a new stock addition was Merck. Merck was a more attractive company than many others in the industry. The stock also had taken a severe beating. It had fallen from a high of $61 a share in 2008, to a measly $32 by early 2011. I examined the fundamentals of Merck starting with a financial ratio analysis (see Table 3.8).

TABLE 3.8 Financial Ratio Analysis

E.P.S.	$3.70
Current Ratio	2.6
Debt/Equity	22%
Interest Cover	7.4
Operating Margin	24%
R.O.E.	21%
Price/Sales	3.2

Source: Standard & Poor's.

My analysis concluded that

- Merck had an excellent management team led by Kenneth Frazer. Mr. Frazer had been a successful attorney within Merck, defending the Vioxx litigation. His focus at Merck now that he was CEO was a return to growth and research and development. He was the perfect candidate to resuscitate Merck.

- Merck had solid liquidity and debt ratings. It had one of the lowest debt ratios (22%) in the sector.
- Merck had a very low revenue base with terrific new drug prospects. Its new drug pipeline was dramatically enhanced by its acquisition of Schering-Plough in 2009. Schering-Plough complemented Merck's lineup of prescription drugs, doubling the number of drugs in late stages of development to 18 and expanded its push into cancer and brain therapies. Merck also projected $3.5 billion in yearly savings after 2011.
- With its pipeline of new drugs, Merck had one of the highest expected growth rates in the industry; 8% annual earnings per share (E.P.S.) growth through 2016.
- Merck was trading at a P/S ratio of 3.2. This is one of the lowest P/S ratios within its industry. Its historical P/S range over the past 10 years was 3.1 to 7.5. Thus, I felt safe purchasing Merck at its lower valuation range.
- Merck paid an annual dividend of $1.52 per share, a 4.5% annual yield for a patient investor.

I purchased Merck for my clients at an average cost of $33.50 a share.

CHAPTER 4

The Energy Sector

Drill for oil? You mean drill into the ground to try and find oil? You're crazy!

Anonymous to Edwin Drake, 1859

The energy sector is composed of five major industry groups: integrated oil and gas, oil and gas equipment and service, oil and gas drilling, oil and gas exploration and production, and refining and marketing firms. Oil and natural gas are considered to be "commodities." That is, they are basic materials that are available from a wide variety of suppliers and whose prices are intensely subject to the laws of supply and demand. The prices of virtually all commodities, from copper to pork bellies, had been very low throughout the late 1990s and early 2000s. This has dramatically changed over the past decade as the price of oil has increased above $100 a barrel.

In general, the energy sector today is one of (1) heightened competition, (2) increased capacity and higher operating costs, both driven by dramatic leaps forward in technology, and therefore (3) heightened demand from emerging nations such as China, Brazil, and India. The result is restricted supply, typically leading to higher prices. Energy stocks represent a 13.2% weighting of the benchmark S&P 500 Index. The sector has delivered exceptional investment returns over the 24-year period ending

December 31, 2010. As demonstrated in Chapter 2, this category's return, as measured by my data, was a 10.5% annual return. Future performance of the energy sector will be determined by global demand and future energy needs. Part of the case for a separate allocation to energy stocks is that they are a real asset that benefits a portfolio in inflationary times. From 1970 to 1981, a period considered to be one of rising inflation, energy stocks dramatically outperformed broad-market indices.[1]

I believe there are four main characteristics that favor owning energy firms:

- Global demand for energy services will continue to accelerate.
- Future supplies of oil will be harder to find and more costly to extract.
- Energy firms have strong financial characteristics, including rising dividends.
- Energy firms represent a strong inflation hedge in a diversified portfolio.

The combination of these factors should enable these stocks to generate the returns necessary to make this sector very attractive for long-term investors.

Global Demand

World oil consumption has been increasing at a rate of 2.2% per year since 2000 and reached 87.6 million barrels per day in the first quarter of 2011. Although the United States currently accounts for one-quarter of world consumption, growth in oil use has been lower in the United States than in the rest of the world for the past 40 years. The Energy Information Administration (EIA) projects that world oil demand will grow 2.7% per year through 2020. Oil consumption in Asian countries will be equal to that in the United States by 2020. China, India, and South Korea will more than double their oil consumption over this period. Similarly, demand in Central and South America is expected to double. Oil demand and price are set to grow strongly over the next 25 years despite environmental policies, essentially dooming climate-change goals, according to the International Energy Agency.

Slightly more than a third of the new demand would come from China's appetite for energy. The IEA forecasts the price of crude oil to increase 88% by 2035 to $113 a barrel in inflation-adjusted dollars. Under the calculations that take into account climate-change pledges made under the Copenhagen Accord in 2010, fossil fuels will still account for more than half of the increase in total energy demand, with oil to remain the dominant fuel. The IEA forecasts demand for oil to rise by 18% between 2009 and 2035, driven by developing countries, with nearly half the increase accounted for by China alone. Global demand for oil would total 99.0 million barrels per day in 2035, or 15.0 million barrels per day more than in 2009, and all of the increase would come from outside the OECD area of advanced economies.

Future Supplies

The future of energy is of enormous importance. The global energy market is intricate and the analysis of it is complex. Most of the known world reserves exist in regions and countries that are not stable. Consumers cannot control where oil reserves exist, and the geostrategic risks are not likely to change in the near future. Oil (and all other fossil fuels) occurs in finite amounts on planet Earth. Therefore, assuming demand continues to expand rather than diminish, some point in time will occur when the rate at which fossil fuels can be extracted will peak and thereafter can only decline. That is the point to which "peak oil" refers. In contrast, "renewable energy" refers to solar, wind, hydro, and geothermal sources for generating electricity, all of which are dependent on the recurring energy we get from the sun or from heat stored underground. The supply, in theory, is virtually infinite and their production can be expanded almost infinitely so long as the planet remains roughly as it is today climatically. In addition, there are "hybrid renewables—products such as ethanol and hydrogen. These depend in some ways on a renewable input such as corn or cellulose, but also require a substantial input of processing that, at least at present, consumes a good deal of fossil fuels.

Technology can impact both supply and demand for oil. The speed at which a given oil deposit can be extracted and what sorts of mineral deposits can be used as a source of oil are affected by technology. For example, the oil sands in Canada and Venezuela are now considered a major source of oil in the world, but only 10 years ago, before the technology for turning the oil sands into oil was perfected and before the price of oil was high enough to make the higher cost oil sands production profitable, the oil sands were not considered to be a reliable source of oil.

Pessimistic assumptions and high economic growth would put the 50% exhaustion point of total oil reserves at 2020. While ExxonMobil, BP, and the other major oil firms are undeniably huge enterprises, the vast majority of oil reserves are still owned by various national governments through their state-owned oil companies. In fact, the governments of such major producers as Mexico, Venezuela, and Saudi Arabia control about 90% of the reserves and 69% of the production of the world's oil and gas. Consequently, political considerations will continue to have intensive influence on the energy business. Satisfying the massive surges in the demand for oil projected in recent studies requires massive investments to build new infrastructure and finance new technologies. The IEA projects that with world oil demand rising by 60% by 2030, the world energy market would need $16 trillion of cumulative investment between 2008 and 2030 or $580 billion a year. Even this estimate is based on unrealistically low estimates of investment cost and outdated assumptions about the sophisticated exploration, development, and production technology and equipment needed in modern oil fields. Yet it still requires vast transfers of capital. This capital should flow to the major oil and service firms over the next decade.

Strong Financial Position

A strong financial position is always important to an energy firm, as the capital requirements for exploration and development are very high. Strong balance sheets with low debt levels, high return on equity, and significant free cash flow generation are key drivers to success in the energy sector. The generation of positive cash flow is particularly important in the current market environment, given that funding for more technologically challenging oil projects will become more critical. Energy firms now maintain strong balance sheets and diversified business mixes that involve energy production, refining, and chemicals. Exxon has $30 billion in net cash (cash less debt) and is likely to produce almost $50 billion of after-tax profit in 2011. One potential plus for the oil majors in the next few years is that refining margins, which have collapsed, could reverse course.

Strong Inflation Hedge

Part of the case for a separate allocation to energy stocks is the fact the sector will outperform and will provide an investor diversification during period of inflationary times. Chen and Pinsky [2002][2] found that during a period from 1970 to 1981 energy stocks dramatically outperformed broad-market stocks.

In the first nine months of 1979, average annual inflation jumped to 10.75%. This dramatic rise was due to a new round of oil price increases. The energy sector also excelled in this period of booming commodity prices and rising inflation. In 1979, energy stocks were up 68%. The sector also excelled in 1980, rising an additional 83%. Evidence from the 1970s supports the contention that energy stocks benefit most during periods of rising inflation and oil prices.

Sub-Sector Analysis

The Integrated Oil and Gas Industry

The integrated oil and gas industry represents 8% of the benchmark S&P 500, and the greater part of the overall sector weight. Major international energy companies are engaged in the diverse aspects of oil and gas operations, including crude oil and gas exploration, production, manufacturing, refining, marketing, and transportation. Major oil companies include international integrated oil companies that are involved in every aspect of the oil business from exploration and production to refining and marketing. Most are busy in the manufacture and sale of petrochemical products as well. Major companies include ExxonMobil, PetroChina, Total, and Chevron (see Table 4.1).

The Oil and Gas Services Industry

Companies involved in the oil and gas services sub-sector manufacture oil field equipment or provide service to the major international oil firms. Servicing companies provide drilling and exploration support by means of offshore and onshore drilling consulting as well as related oil well and contracting services, including seismic surveys, equipment and tool rental, pumping and processing services, and inspection and contracting

TABLE 4.1 Major Oil and Gas Integrated Firms

	Industry	Market Cap
ExxonMobil Corp.	Oil and Gas Integrated	407,042.46
PetroChina Co., Ltd.	Oil and Gas Integrated	255,424.08
Petroleo Brasileiro SA	Oil and Gas Integrated	225,278.46
Royal Dutch Shell PLC	Oil and Gas Integrated	220,276.02
Chevron Corp.	Oil and Gas Integrated	207,479.98
BP Oil PLC	Oil and Gas Integrated	142,665.14
Total SA	Oil and Gas Integrated	132,416.15
Eni SpA	Oil and Gas Integrated	107,623.99
ConocoPhilips	Oil and Gas Integrated	102,677.12
Suncor Energy, Inc.	Oil and Gas Integrated	65,684.38
Imperial Oil, Ltd.	Oil and Gas Integrated	41,391.89
Marathon Oil Corp.	Oil and Gas Integrated	38,004.16
Hess Corp.	Oil and Gas Integrated	26,704.13

Source: Standard & Poor's.

services. The major issue confronting the industry is the outdated energy infrastructure. This energy space has lacked major new investment for the past two decades. Investment has been lacking because producers have emphasized return on capital rather than production growth. Production growth is now on the forefront as the major oil companies try to reduce their exposure to the low-margin refining business. Therefore, the demand for exploration and drilling activity by major oil and refining companies is due to expand exponentially. The oil and gas services industry is also closely eyeing a recent proposal from Democrats calling for the reduction of billions of dollars worth of tax breaks. Democrats also proposed an excise tax on some leases in the Gulf of Mexico. Nothing has been passed yet, but the ongoing proposals are worth tracking for investors within the industry. Major players include Schlumberger, Halliburton, and Baker Hughes (see Table 4.2).

TABLE 4.2 Major Oil and Gas Services Firms

	Industry	Market Cap
Schlumberger, Ltd.	Oil and Gas Services	114,946.40
Halliburton Co.	Oil and Gas Services	45,887.91
Baker Hughes, Inc.	Oil and Gas Services	31,928.27
Weatherford International, Ltd.	Oil and Gas Services	14,642.66
Cameron International Corp.	Oil and Gas Services	11,606.60
FMC Technologies, Inc.	Oil and Gas Services	10,591.20

Source: Standard & Poor's.

The Oil and Gas Drilling Industry

Drilling companies physically drill and pump oil out of the ground. The drilling industry has always been classified as highly skilled. The people with the skills and expertise to operate equipment are in high demand, which means that for an oil company to have these people on staff all the time can cost a lot. For this reason, most drilling companies are simply contractors who are hired by oil and gas producers for a specified period of time. Oil and gas drillers usually charge oil producers on a daily work rate. These rates fluctuate depending on the location, the type of rig employed, and the market conditions. There are plenty of research firms that publish this information. Higher day rates are great for drilling companies, but for refiners and distribution

TABLE 4.3 Major Oil and Gas Drilling Firms

	Industry	Market Cap
National Oilwell	Oil and Gas Drilling	30,825.41
Transocean, Ltd.	Oil and Gas Drilling	22,034.18
Seadrill, Ltd.	Oil and Gas Drilling	15,766.41
Noble Corp.	Oil and Gas Drilling	10,477.52
Diamond Offshore Drilling	Oil and Gas Drilling	10,128.12

Source: Standard & Poor's.

companies this results in lower margins unless energy prices are rising at the same rate (see Table 4.4).

The Oil and Gas Exploration and Production Industry

Firms in the oil and gas exploration and production industry acquire, develop, and operate oil and gas field properties. Products of the industry include crude oil, natural gas, and hydrocarbon liquids. Competitors within the industry include both independent oil and gas producers and large integrated energy companies. The integrated energy companies also have operations in fuel refining, oil and gas marketing, and chemical production. As such, their extraction operations have a ready consumer for what they produce. The industry consists of companies that are engaged in the exploration and extraction of crude petroleum and natural gas. The industry is also engaged in recovering butane, ethane, and natural liquefied petroleum gases from oil and gas fields. The oil and gas exploration and production industry excludes exploration services on a contract basis, which are classified in oil-related services and equipment.

TABLE 4.4 Major Oil and Gas Exploration/Production Firms

	Industry	Market Cap
Occidental Petroleum Corp.	Oil and Gas E&P	86,628.05
Apache Corp.	Oil and Gas E&P	47,259.79
Anadarko Petroleum Corp.	Oil and Gas E&P	39,134.98
Devon Energy Corp.	Oil and Gas E&P	35,252.82
EOG Resources	Oil and Gas E&P	29,031.25
Encana Corp.	Oil and Gas E&P	24,995.21
Talisman Energy, Inc.	Oil and Gas E&P	21,507.23
Chesapeake Energy Corp.	Oil and Gas E&P	20,459.96
Noble Energy, Inc.	Oil and Gas E&P	16,303.72
Southwestern Energy Co.	Oil and Gas E&P	15,088.45

Source: Standard & Poor's.

The industry also excludes exploration and production with substantial refining operations, which are classified in the integrated oil and gas sub-sector. Major firms within this industry include Occidental, Apache, and Devon Energy (see Table 4.4).

The Oil and Gas Refining and Marketing Industry

Firms in the oil and gas refining and marketing industry are engaged in downstream activities, which include refining and selling crude oil products such as gasoline, jet fuel, heating oil, motor oil, and lubricants. These companies include Valero, Sunoco, and Tessoro. Most of the firms in this industry are of a smaller market capitalization. Marketing is the delivery of products to end users through retail gasoline stations (see Table 4.5).

TABLE 4.5 Major Oil and Gas Refining Firms

	Industry	Market Cap
Valero Corp.	Oil and Gas Refining and Marketing	15,351.01

Source: Standard & Poor's.

Investing in the Energy Sector

The energy sector should account for the third-highest weight of your stock portfolio, approximately 10 to 15%. The sector is greatly valued due to its excellent long-term performance results along with inflation protection. The sector maintains a low correlation with the other major sectors. Energy stocks can also reduce the volatility of your overall stock portfolio due to the low betas of many of the major oil and gas integrated firms such as Exxon. Here are some guidelines:

- Choose only those firms that are No. 1 or No. 2 in their respective industries or in a particular market segment.

- Ensure that you have exposure to energy stocks that have a high correlation to the price of oil (oil equipment and service companies and drillers).
- Select firms that have strong fundamentals, strong management, and strong product positioning.
- Select companies of a large size (5 billion market cap >). Attempt to add to your portfolio when energy stocks are out of favor.

Stock Selection Case Studies

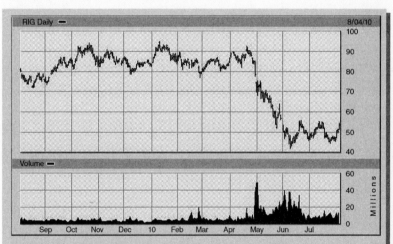

FIGURE 4.1 Case Study No. 3: Transocean, July 2010
Source: Charts provided by Commodity Systems, Inc. (CSI) 2012.

The 2010 Gulf disaster that killed 11 workers and spilled millions of gallons of oil into the Gulf of Mexico did not squeeze just British Petroleum's stock but the stock of any oil firm that had ties to the disaster. This included offshore driller Transocean, which owned and operated the Deepwater Horizon rig (which BP had leased). The Deepwater

(continued)

(*continued*)

Horizon was insured for $560 million—already paid to Transocean—but investors feared the company would be held liable for billions more in clean-up costs and restitution. The company's stock had taken a remarkable beating since the Deepwater Horizon explosion. Shares of Transocean (NYSE: RIG), which owned and operated the rig, showed little change for the first few days following the explosion, but as the scope of the disaster became clear and investors began to suspect possible errors by the company, the potential financial responsibility for the explosion took its toll. The shares of Transocean had fallen by more than 50% from $92.03 on April 20 to the mid $40s.

Earnings per share at Transocean, which had climbed from $.67 in 2000 to $14.14 in 2007, were expected to fall by 30% in 2010 as a result of the disaster. Analysts were cutting their ratings. At $45 a share, investors were discounting the worst in Transocean stock. I examined the fundamentals of Transocean in detail, starting with my favorite ratios pulled from the balance sheet and income statement (see Table 4.6).

I drew the following conclusions:

- Transocean was an industry leader in the oil and natural gas drilling sector. The company had the highest operating and net margins within its industry.
- Transocean had a strong management team led by industry veteran Robert Long.
- Although Transocean had a relatively weak interest coverage ratio, the firm had solid cash flow and a reasonable current ratio. Therefore, I felt that the balance sheet could support further weakness within the oil and gas industry.

TABLE 4.6 Fundamentals of Transocean Ratios

2009 E.P.S.	$10.99
Current Ratio	2.34
Working Cap	6.3m
Debt/Equity	33%
Interest Cover	3.5
Operating Margin	53%
Net Margin	18%
Price/Sales	2.3
FCF Yield	10%

Source: Standard & Poor's.

- Despite a very poor 2010, Transocean still earned a profit. On a price/sales basis, Transocean was trading at a 2.3 ratio. During the past 10 years, Transocean had an average P/S ratio of 4.9. Its P/S range, equally important, was 2.1 to 10.8. Therefore, on a relative basis, Transocean was trading near its historical trough level.
- Transocean had the largest fleet of rigs in the industry (131).
- Transocean had a free cash flow yield of 11%. Although earnings were low, cash flow was much higher due to the large amount of depreciation Transocean carried.

I felt that Transocean presented an excellent investment opportunity. Considering the price of Transocean had fallen so dramatically, I also felt the downside was limited due to the low P/S ratio. One factor limiting risk was that Transocean, in addition to limiting its liability for the oil spill, stood to make a $270 million profit from the insurance on Deepwater Horizon, having insured it for more than it was worth. If the recovery in the Gulf took hold in the next 18 months and liability was limited to estimates, the potential upside in RIG was well above $100.

(*continued*)

(*continued*)

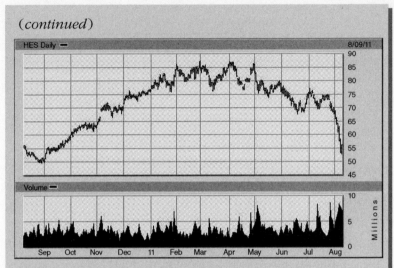

FIGURE 4.2 Case Study No. 4: Hess Oil, August 2011
Source: Charts provided by Commodity Systems, Inc. (CSI) 2012.

During the summer of 2011, the U.S. economy started showing signs of weakness, including a GDP growth rate below
2%. The stock market tanked in early August as the reper-
cussions of the European debt problem impacted the United
States. Economists also started ratcheting down growth
expectations for the second half of 2011 while also reducing
the projections for the price of oil. Secondarily, in June the
Obama administration released 30 million barrels of crude
oil from the U.S. Strategic Petroleum Reserve, while partner
countries in the International Energy Agency also released
another 30 million barrels. Within hours of the announce-
ment, oil's per-barrel price fell more than $8 to the lowest
level since February. We felt that the release of crude was a
political stunt and would not result in altering the long term
dynamics of the oil and natural gas industries. We had maintained a small position in Hess Oil during 2011. Hess is one
of the premier integrated oil firms involved in exploration
and production on several continents. The firm also

TABLE 4.7 Hess Ratios

2011 E.P.S. (expected)	$5.15
Debt/Equity	24%
Time Interest Earned	13.3
Operating Margin	17.5%
Net Margin	7%
Price/Sales	0.58
Price/Earnings	9.1
P.E.G. Ratio	0.9

Source: Standard & Poor's.

maintains refining and marketing primarily on the U.S. East Coast. Our attraction to Hess is based on the firm's exploration and development in the North Dakota Bakken Shale area. Hess was generating 20% plus average annual production growth at North Dakota Bakken oil shale properties.

Hess also increased its exposure to the Bakken area through acquisitions. In late 2010, the firm acquired 85,000 net acres via an all-stock purchase of American Oil & Gas and another 167,000 acquired via the all-cash purchase of TRZ Energy. Hess now had a leading position in the Bakken of more than 900,000 net acres. Hess had projected to boost Bakken production from 17,000 barrels of oil equivalent per day (boe/d) to over 60,000 boe/d by 2015. Hess also had an intriguing oil field being developed off the coast of Ghana, in which it had a 90% stake. We thought the firm offered one of the best risk/reward characteristics within the energy sector.

I examined the fundamentals of Hess in detail, starting with my favorite ratios pulled from the balance sheet and income statement: Please refer to Table 4.7.

(*continued*)

(*continued*)

I arrived at the following conclusions:

- Hess was an early leader in natural gas and oil exploration within the Bakken area, providing for excellent growth in earnings and revenue over the next five years.
- Despite the acquisitions of several promising oil and gas properties over the past several years, Hess actually improved its balance sheet. The firm has reduced its debt capitalization ratio from nearly 60% at the start of the decade to 24% by 2011.
- In the first quarter of 2011, Hess had reported a profit of $929 million, or $2.74 a share, up from $538 million, or $1.65 a share, a year earlier. Revenue had jumped an impressive 14% to $10.52 billion.
- Hess's stock had fallen by $30 a share from early May 2011 until the beginning of August, a drop of 35%. The stock now traded at only nine times earnings based on our estimate of $7.65 E.P.S. for year 2011. The P.E.G. ratio was one of the best within the industry.
- Hess also traded at a P/S ratio of 0.58, toward the lower end of the company's historical range.
- Hess had over $2 billion cash on its balance sheet and had in place a credit of an additional $4 billion available. Thus, the firm's capital and fund-raising capability was exemplary.

I felt that as with Transocean, Hess presented an exceptional investment opportunity within the energy space. We added to our position in Hess on this pullback and set a target price of $100 per share by the end of 2012.

CHAPTER 5

The Consumer Staples Sector

The consumer is not a moron. She is your wife.

David Ogilvy

The U.S. consumer staples industry accounts for a major portion of the U.S. economy, amounting to expenditures of $1.6 trillion in 2010. The sector is composed of companies whose primary lines of business are food, beverages, tobacco, and other household items. Examples of these companies include Procter & Gamble, Colgate Palmolive, and Hershey. These companies have historically been characterized as non-cyclical in nature as compared with their close relative, the consumer cyclicals sector. Unlike other areas of the economy, even during economically slow times (in theory), the demand for the products made by consumer staples companies does not slow down. Some staples (e.g., discount foods, liquor, and tobacco) actually may see increased demand during slow economic times. In line with the non-cyclical nature of the demand for their products, the demand for these stocks tends to move in similar patterns.

This sector represents 10.6% of the market capitalization of the S&P 500, making it the fifth-largest sector. The sector has delivered exceptional investment returns over the 24-year period ending December 31, 2010. As demonstrated in Chapter 2, the category's return, as measured by my data, was a 11.4%

annual return. As with health care, the sector offers very strong defensive characteristics. I believe there are three key characteristics that make owning many consumer staples stocks beneficial:

- A consistent, predictable record of profit growth
- Emerging market opportunities
- Excellent financial capabilities and reliable products

The combination of these features should enable this sector to generate the earnings that makes these holdings attractive for long-term investors.

Consistent Profit Growth

One of the true attractions of the consumer staples sector is the consistency of earnings growth. The rate of earnings growth has surpassed market averages over a number of decades. Solid earnings growth is driven principally by brand adherence, which protects market share and pricing power. Steadfast margin expansion stemming from the predictability of demand should also assist staples firms to continue to meet future earnings targets. The uniformity of earnings growth historically has differentiated the consumer sector from other more economically sensitive sectors. Stability and reliability are driven by the elemental nature of the products, such as detergents, toothpaste, cigarettes, soft drinks, juices, toilet paper, cosmetics, and beer, which are purchased on a weekly basis and are in most circumstances used daily.

Because these products are essentially indispensable in nature, demand is much less elastic than in durable product areas such as automobiles, appliances, and home furnishings. Although consumers can clear their pantries before repurchasing or cut down modestly on consumption, demand is relatively established for these frequently used foodstuffs and other products. The generally low price point of these items relative to big-ticket purchases also makes consumer staples products less of a target of household budget cuts during tough economic times.

Global Growth Opportunities

Many staples companies will likely preserve strong growth rates because of the vast global opportunities to sell their products, especially to consumers in the emerging markets. The emerging markets provide a multi-decade growth opening for well-capitalized multinational staples companies. China and India, in particular, are in the midst of an extended industrialization and urbanization process. From 1998 through 2007, for example, the economies of India and China grew at rates more than twice the rate of the U.S. economy.[1] With 85 percent of the world's population living outside the developed world, emerging market economies are projected to become significantly more important contributors to global gross domestic product (GDP). Local utilization rates have accelerated in emerging markets, as more and more households have entered the middle class—a dynamic that is impacting growth across all consumer industries. Consumer product companies are one of the most apparent beneficiaries, as an increase in disposable income allows for a higher standard of living in formerly undeveloped regions. Food product firms are a beneficiary as well, as diets have broadened to contain more animal proteins, driving significant demand for more Western products. Over the next decade, there will be a dramatic rise of the emerging middle class, measured by the growth in the number of households with disposable income of $5,000–$15,000. The IMF has found that this segment of the population in emerging economies (including China, India, and Brazil) more than doubled between 2000 and 2010, and it is expected to continue to rise at a rapid rate throughout the next decade.

As the economies of emerging markets are expected to play a greater role in global equity returns, investors will want more exposure to large consumer product firms that will benefit from this movement. Because the products sold in the emerging markets are largely the same products consumed in developed markets, the consumer staples firms can also enjoy tremendous economies of scale and enhanced profitability.

Strong Financials and Reliable Products

A strong financial position is always important to a corporation, but in more challenging economic environments like those of today, it becomes critical to firms that are trying to grow. Strong balance sheets with low debt levels, high return on equity, and significant free cash flow generation are key drivers of our affinity toward the staples sector. Nearly every large firm that competes on a global scale maintains low debt, high returns on equity, and strong cash flow. The production of positive cash flow is particularly vital in the current market environment inasmuch as funding for companies across all sectors has become sparse during the credit crunch era. Brand loyalty, pricing power, global product appeal, and relatively unwavering demand for products are among the primary factors that permit staples companies to generate consistent cash flow. This can then be used to fund operations through an assortment of stages in a business cycle. For example, if revenues can grow 5% on an ongoing basis, but cost of products is limited to the low single digits, global firms can easily deliver secure margin expansion. Multinational firms such as Coca-Cola, Procter & Gamble, and Nestlé have shown a high capability to price effectively while expanding margins during economic cycles.

The large global consumer firms also have a high degree of commitment to innovation in their product categories. Because these firms have a number-one market share position in many staple classes, the firms can meet the expense of further research and development. Successful originality protects and enlarges market share and frequently serves as an apparatus for pricing power. Consumer staples firms also have demonstrated un-swerving staying power and are generally not vulnerable to ob-solescence. Whereas in some industries, such as technology, it is difficult to project whether the goods will be germane in 15 years, for most staples products, there is a high degree of certainty that the world will be in need of similar products for decades to come.

The Consumer Staples Retailing Industry

The consumer staples retailing industry comprises nearly one-third of the staples sector and accounts for 3% of the overall benchmark S&P 500 Index. These companies sell products di-rectly to the consumer that are necessary for daily living, not for a discretionary need. These products usually represent a repeat purchase, no matter the economic situation. Unlike other areas of the staples sector, little has remained the same over the past decade within the retailing industry. One of the few similarities with today is that Wal-Mart was ranked the top retailer in the world back then and it still holds that distinction. Other than Wal-Mart's dominance, there's little about today's environment that looks like the mid-1990s. Saturated home markets, fierce competition, and restrictive legislation have relentlessly pushed major food and staples retailers into the market share mode. Large new competitors have pushed into the industry, including Target, Costco, and Sam's Club. Target is a newer competitor in the market, gaining a large amount of market share during the 2000s. The other major trend within the retailing industry is the advancement of the pharmacy, specialty, and dollar stores. Wal-greens, CVS, Whole Foods, Dollar General, and Dollar Tree have

TABLE 5.1 Major Staples Retailing Firms

	Industry	Market Cap
Wal-Mart Stores, Inc.	Staples Retailing	189,324.00
CVS Corp.	Staples Retailing	50,644.30
Costco Wholesale Corp.	Staples Retailing	37,756.18
Walgreens Co.	Staples Retailing	35,756.11
Target Corp.	Staples Retailing	35,704.62
The Kroger Co.	Staples Retailing	15,315.38
Whole Foods Market, Inc.	Staples Retailing	11,619.88
Dollar General Corp.	Staples Retailing	11,338.98
Dollar Tree Stores, Inc.	Staples Retailing	8,407.77
Safeway, Inc.	Staples Retailing	7,411.31
Delhaize Group	Staples Retailing	7,304.86
Family Dollar Stores, Inc.	Staples Retailing	6,509.88

Source: Standard & Poor's.

all carved out lucrative market share away from many of the major industry players during the past decade (see Table 5.1).

The Food Products Industry

The food products industry includes packaged foods, meats, and agriculture products. The major categories can be broadly grouped into foodstuffs and an assortment of ornamental products. Specific foods include fruits, cereal, and vegetables. Also included within this group are fibers, which include wool, cotton, and silk. Food safety has been a hot topic for some time now, but it is gaining even more attention with the recent signing of the Food Safety Modernization Act (FSMA), which is regarded as the most comprehensive reform of food supply oversight since the late 1930s. The FSMA, signed into law on Jan. 4, 2011, focuses heavily on deterrence rather than response and is designed to reduce the incidence of food-related illnesses in the United States. The Food and Drug Administration (FDA) now has extensive authority over food companies, excluding USDA-regulated meat, poultry, and dairy producers.

Historically, developed countries such as the United States have been the biggest producers of food products. However, there has been a modification, with China, Russia, and India increasing production capabilities. All three are now ranked in the top five in production of wheat. Additionally, food purchases in developing countries are shifting from staple foods rich in carbohydrates to more costly foods such as meat and dairy products, indicating the substantial growth promise of developing countries versus developed economies. This theme is visible even on the consumption front. According to the food and beverage industry, about 58% of food produced is consumed by developing countries. This is expected to climb to 72% by 2050, supported by the fact that 37% of the world's population currently lives in China and India. Top companies that stand to benefit from this trend include Kraft, General Mills, Sysco, and Archer Daniels (see Table 5.2).

TABLE 5.2 **Major Food Product Companies**

	Industry	Market Cap
Kraft Foods, Inc.	Food Products	62,281.55
General Mills, Inc.	Food Products	24,388.71
Archer Daniels Midland	Food Products	20,488.90
Kellogg Co.	Food Products	20,288.39
H.J. Heinz Co.	Food Products	17,372.22
Sysco Co.	Food Products	16,280.98
Hershey Foods Corp.	Food Products	13,289.05
Sara Lee Corp.	Food Products	11,462.12
ConAgra Foods, Inc.	Food Products	10,894.30
Campbell Soup Co.	Food Products	10,852.88
J.M. Smucker Co.	Food Products	9,150.24

Source: Standard & Poor's.

The Beverages Industry

The beverages industry includes companies that produce, market, and bottle alcoholic and nonalcoholic beverages, carbonated drinks, juices, energy/sports drinks, water, coffee, and tea. Vying to slack the thirsts of the dry mouths of the world, beverage manufacturers are in stiff competition. In the kingdom of nonalcoholic drinks, carbonated soft drinks have long reigned. The industry is dominated by three major players: Coca-Cola is emperor of the soft drink empire, followed by PepsiCo and Cadbury. Among alcoholic beverage producers, consolidation has given the industry three giant players: AmBev, Annheuser Busch InBev, and SAB Miller. The notoriously high costs of distribution and brand building have created huge barriers to entry within the beverage industry.

Consolidation should continue throughout the next decade as firms continue to build market share and demonstrate their ability to reduce costs. The global middle class will be a principal target for all beverage companies as the developed markets become passé. The global middle class is rising faster than expected, in numbers and in wealth. In 2009, 70 million people joined the emerging-market middle class, with incomes between $6,000 and $30,000.[2] Given the rise in incomes, consumer awareness regarding a healthier lifestyle is also having an impact. This path is displayed by PepsiCo's focus on its good-for-you product line, which currently generates more than $10 billion in sales through brands such as Tropicana, Naked Juice, and Aquafina. PepsiCo's tactical plan is to nurture its nutrition business to $25 billion by 2020.

In alcoholic beverages, the industry is also feeling the effects of lifestyle. Today's wine and liquor drinkers are more prosperous and health conscious. The combination of these developments has resulted in a slight reduction in overall alcohol consumption in many regions of the world. But it is also driving demand upstream for premium alcoholic drinks, from

TABLE 5.3 Major Beverage Companies

	Industry	Market Cap
The Coca-Cola Co.	Beverages—Soft Drinks	159,629.71
PepsiCo, Inc.	Beverages—Soft Drinks	104,072.13
AmBev	Beverages—Brewers	99,260.74
Anheuser-Busch InBev SA	Beverages—Brewers	95,133.51
SABMiller PLC	Beverages—Brewers	62,844.44
Diageo PLC	Beverages—Distillers/ Distilleries	51,755.84
Heineken N.V.	Beverages—Brewers	34,421.92
Dr Pepper Snapple	Beverages—Soft Drinks	8,934.22
Molson Coors Brewing Co.	Beverages—Brewers	8,700.84

Source: Standard & Poor's.

high-quality wines to first-class beers. Premium liquors such as whiskey and rum are also becoming increasingly trendy as emerging-market customers trade up to higher-end drinks. This has resulted in increased margins for many of the large alcoholic beverage firms. However, the move into these markets is costly for all the major beverage firms. For example, over the past 10 years, the Coca-Cola Company has reported in annual reports investing more than $5 billion on the African continent, and the firm plans to invest another $12 billion by 2020. In this case, the spending is paying off. Coca-Cola recently forecast a doubling of worldwide revenues to $200 billion over the next decade, thanks to another billion people expected to join the middle class by 2020 (see Table 5.3).

The Household Products Industry

The household products industry consists of companies engaged in the manufacturing of non-durable goods such as cleaning products, detergents, disinfectants, brooms, mops, towels and rags, and disposable plates and cutlery. Consolidation within the household products industry has continued throughout this decade, and further acquisitions are expected for the achievement of economies of scale and simultaneous top-line growth. The household products industry is mature overall, but product innovation, brand awareness, and intelligent acquisitions can still spark healthy profit growth. Distribution of consumer products through mass merchandisers is one of the major industry shifts, but there is concern over the international exposure of several of the larger companies. Many of the firm's profits are now tied to the fortune of currency movements. As with the beverage industry, emerging economies are a big part of the future for these firms.

Procter & Gamble has maintained an ambitious goal of adding one billion consumers to its global business by 2015, driven largely by growth in emerging markets. Procter & Gamble set a goal of 70% global household penetration—up from 62% in 2010—by 2015. Nestlé produces over 100 different products that are aggressively sold to the emerging-market countries. In 2010, Nestlé's food and beverage sales in the emerging markets achieved over 15% growth and accounted for over one-third of the firm's overall sales (see Table 5.4).

TABLE 5.4 Major Household Product Firms

	Industry	Market Cap
Nestlé SA	Household Product	206,656.65
Procter & Gamble Co.	Household Product	179,340.63
Unilever NV	Household Product	100,184.16
Colgate-Palmolive Co.	Household Product	42,836.89
Kimberly-Clark Corp.	Household Product	26,676.42
Estee Lauder Cos.	Household Product	21,078.76
Avon Products, Inc.	Household Product	12,342.09
Clorox Co.	Household Product	9,914.78
Church & Dwight Co.	Household Product	6,038.51
Energizer Holdings, Inc.	Household Product	5,549.50

Source: Standard & Poor's.

The Tobacco Industry

The tobacco industry consists of companies engaged in the growth, preparation for sale, shipment, advertisement, and allotment of tobacco and tobacco-related products. It is a global industry; as tobacco can grow in any warm, moist environment, which means it can be farmed on all continents except Antarctica. Tobacco is a commodity product similar in economic terms to foodstuffs in that the price is fairly inelastic. The price does vary by specific species grown, the total quantity on the market ready for sale, the area where it was grown, the health of the plants, and other characteristics individual to product quality. Laws around the world now often have some restrictions on smoking, but still 5.5 trillion cigarettes are smoked each year. Taxes are often heavily imposed on tobacco. The industry has relied on international markets for most of the growth in the past decade. Phillip Morris International, which was spun off from Altria in early 2008, sells cigarettes and other tobacco products in over 160 countries with the bulk of its growth coming from the emerging markets (see Table 5.5).

INVESTING IN THE STAPLES SECTOR   The staples sector should represent 20 to 30% of your overall portfolio. This large weight reflects the fact that the sector provides an exceptional

TABLE 5.5 Major Tobacco Companies

	Industry	Market Cap
Philip Morris International, Inc.	Tobacco	128,241.07
British American Tobacco PLC	Tobacco	93,060.69
Altria Group, Inc.	Tobacco	55,181.69
Imperial Tobacco Group PLC	Tobacco	35,627.81
Reynolds American, Inc.	Tobacco	21,135.51
Lorillard, Inc.	Tobacco	16,136.63

Source: Standard & Poor's.

long-term investment return with terrific defensive characteristics. This sector will also perform best during a recession and offset losses in the more economically sensitive sectors—energy, financials, and technology. Stock selection within the staples sector should concentrate on the large consumer firms such as Proctor & Gamble, Coca Cola, and Kraft. The balance of money should be diversified between the major other sub-sectors listed previously. The following guidelines should be observed:

- Select companies of a large size (5 billion market cap >).
- Favor industry leaders within each sub-sector.
- Attempt to add to your portfolio sub-sectors that are out of favor (see stock selection case studies).
- Add to staples when the economy is near the end of an economic boom. If the Federal Reserve starts raising interest rates, increase exposure to both staples and health care.

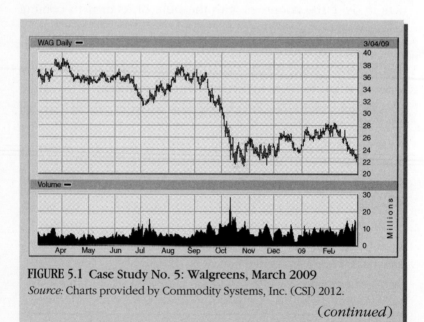

FIGURE 5.1 Case Study No. 5: Walgreens, March 2009
Source: Charts provided by Commodity Systems, Inc. (CSI) 2012.

(continued)

The subprime and banking meltdown of 2008 had a dramatic impact on the share prices of retail and consumer stocks. From October 2007 to March 2009, the retail exchange traded fund SPDR, S&P Consumer Staples (XLP), dropped 33% in value. I sensed the opportunity of a bargain in the bin. Walgreens, a primary holding of the Consumer Staples SPDR ETF, had dropped much farther than that of the index, from a high of $48 a share to just under $23 in a period of 12 months. Analysts were cutting the firm's ratings and earnings estimates in a dramatic fashion. However, the Federal Reserve Bank had initiated a substantial interest-rate reduction campaign. With interest rates on mortgages remaining low and the federal government backing financial companies through the TARP and TALF programs, I felt the economy could pick up steam by 2010 with Walgreens being a primary beneficiary. I examined the fundamentals of Walgreens in detail, starting with my favorite ratios pulled from the balance sheet and income statement (see Table 5.6).

TABLE 5.6 Walgreens Ratios

2008 E.P.S.	$2.02
Current Ratio	1.12
Debt/Equity	28%
Interest Cover	8.2
Operating Margin	11%
Gross Margin	34%
Price/Sales	0.8
FCF Yield	9.3%

Source: Standard & Poor's.

I arrived at the following conclusions:

- Walgreens was the industry leader in the retail industry, outpacing CVS in nearly every measure of efficiency, profitability, and growth rates.

(continued)

(*continued*)

- Walgreens actually increased its operating and gross profit margins during a very difficult 2008. Debt ratios had declined in the previous three years despite the high capital costs of building new stores.
- Walgreens had a very low valuation and an expected growth rate of 12% for the next five years. This compares favorably with its P/E ratio of 12. In 2009, Walgreens still planned to open 80 stores total in the United States and Canada. Walgreens has a dedicated strategy over the next several years that involves expanding within the United States and Canada and also entering Mexico in 2009.
- Walgreens had traded at a price/sales ratio range of 0.6 to 1.7. The current ratio was at the lowest end of the historical spread.
- Walgreens had a very low debt ratio and a strong interest coverage ratio. If the recession got worse during 2009, I felt Walgreens could weather the storm quite well.
- Walgreens had a free cash flow yield of over 9%. This yield was much higher than our minimum 4% criteria at the time (AAA Corporate Bond Yield). Although earnings were low, cash flow was much higher due to the large amount of depreciation Walgreens carried.

I felt that Walgreens presented an excellent long-term investment opportunity. Considering that the price of Walgreens had fallen nearly 50% during the past year, I also felt the downside was limited due to the low historical P/S ratio and the company's strong financial wherewithal. If the economy rebounded during the next two years due to the fiscal stimulus plans promoted by President Obama, Walgreens

(*continued*)

would be one of the primary beneficiaries. I purchased shares in client accounts at $24 a share and set a price target of $50 by 2012. By November 2011, Walgreens share price had reached $32 a share. (see Figure 5.1).

FIGURE 5.2 Case Study No. 6: Coca Cola, July 2010
Source: Charts provided by Commodity Systems, Inc. (CSI) 2012.

During the spring of 2010, the stock market peaked in late April and dropped an additional 15% by the end of the summer. Included in this period was the May 6, 2010 Flash Crash (also known as The Crash of 2:45), in which the Dow Jones Industrial Average plunged about 900 points—or about 9%—only to recover those losses within minutes. It was the second-largest point swing, 1,010.14 points, and the biggest one-day point decline, 998.5 points, on an intraday basis in Dow Jones Industrial Average history. Risk in the market had gone up substantially alongside the start of the financial contagion in Greece. During this period we were examining several companies for purchase, including many stellar

(continued)

(*continued*)

TABLE 5.7 Coca Cola Ratios

2010 E.P.S.	$3.49
Interest Cover	27
Operating Mrgn	31%
Net Mrgn	23%
Price/Sales	3.2
Price/Earnings	14
Return on Equity	28%
FCF Yield	10.8%

Source: Standard & Poor's.

global multinational firms with strong brand names and excellent exposure to emerging markets. Our focus was on the Coca Cola Company. Coca Cola's stock price had fallen from a high of nearly $60 a share to under $50 a share in the market decline. I began to examine Coca Cola starting with my favorite ratios (see Table 5.7).

I arrived at the following conclusions:

- Coca Cola was the number-one firm in the beverage industry with 85% of revenue coming from overseas markets.
- Coca Cola had stellar return on capital, including a return on equity above 25%.
- Despite the financial crisis of 2008, Coca Cola had continued on its growth path. Earnings per share was expected to advance to $3.49 a share in 2010, up from $2.57 in 2007. During the second quarter of 2010, Coca Cola generated 15% earnings growth over the previous year's results.
- Coca Cola traded at a price/sales ratio of just over 3. Over the past 10 years, the price/sales ratio had ranged

(*continued*)

from 2.84 to 6.87. Thus Coca Cola was trading at a low historical valuation. On a price/earnings ratio, the valuation was equally as compelling. Coca Cola traded at a low 14 times 2010 earnings expectations, and only 12.7 times 2011 earnings expectations.

- Coca Cola was generating significant cash. Cash from operations was up 18% on a year-to-date basis. The firm's free cash flow yield was above 10%, one of the highest rates in the sector. The firm also paid out a 3%+ annual dividend, providing for a solid total return while we waited for the market to recover.
- Growth in emerging markets was accelerating. In mid-2010, Eurasia and Africa which saw broad-based growth of 10% in the second quarter and 11% year-to-date. Growth in India was up 22% in the quarter and had a strong 24% year-to-date. Coca Cola was once again becoming a growth company based on the emerging middle class in emerging economies such as India, China, and Brazil.

We purchased Coca Cola for our clients at just under $50 a share. We felt the downside was limited based on Coca Cola's low price/sales ratio and higher than average dividend yield. We felt the upside was well north of $70 a share, based on continued growth in earnings from emerging markets. By the summer of 2011, Coca Cola's stock price had reached our beginning target. We advanced our earnings expectations for the balance of 2011 and 2012 and set a new target price of $80 a share.

CHAPTER 6

The Technology Sector

It has become appallingly obvious that our technology has exceeded our humanity.

Albert Einstein

The technology sector is composed of four major industry groups: computer hardware and storage, semiconductor, software, and Internet companies. This sector is the most volatile in the stock market. The players are sensitive to technological innovations and frequently are subject to competitive changes. Advances in computer processing, network bandwidths, and Internet functioning are the key drivers of the "information age." In 2011, technology stocks represent 18.7% of the benchmark S&P 500 Index. This makes the sector the largest weight within the index. However, this large weight actually discounts the percentage from the beginning of the decade. As of January 1, 2000, the technology weight in the S&P 500 had grown to more than 30%. The NASDAQ exchange, composed mainly of technology companies, dropped 80% in value from March of 2000 to October of 2002. With the substantial drop of the NASDAQ since 2000, technology valuations are now more appropriate and in line with historical averages. Historically, the technology sector has delivered a 9.7% annual return over the 24-year period ending December 31, 2010. I expect that the technology sector will continue to deliver excellent performance over the next decade. Advances in this sector will depend on the continued advancement of the Internet and broadband services, global competition, and cellular technology.

Sectoral Factors

I feel there are three major positive themes for owning technology firms:

- Global demand for the Internet and broadband services
- Government spending
- The strong financial characteristics of technology companies, including high levels of cash assets and strong balance sheets

The combination of these factors should enable these stocks to generate the earnings that make these holdings very attractive for long-term investors.

Broadband Growth

While the 1970s and 1980s will be remembered as the "information age," the 1990s will undoubtedly be singled out in history as the beginning of the "Internet age." The 2000s have become the "broadband age" or even better the "convergence age." The advent of the networked computer was truly revolutionary in terms of information processing, data sharing, and data storage. In the 1990s, the Internet was even more ground-breaking in terms of communications at virtually all levels and in furthering the progress of data sharing, from the personal level to the global enterprise level.

Today, broadband sources such as fiber optic, satellite, and cable modem provide very high-speed access to information and media of all types via the Internet, creating an always-on environment. The result is a widespread convergence of entertainment, telephony, and computerized information. Data, voice, and video are being delivered to a rapidly evolving array of Internet appliances—tablets, wireless devices (including cellular telephones), and desktop computers. Such a high-speed optical connection is the equivalent of dozens of streaming video files running at once. Starting with today's very rapid implementation of cable modem access to U.S. homes, increasingly faster broadband is already altering the technological nature of the U.S. home as well as the office. The boom in usage of mobile broadband and mobile computing applications through smartphones will continue to accelerate for the foreseeable future.

According to the Cisco VNI Forecast (2011), global mobile data traffic grew 2.6-fold in 2010, nearly tripling for the third year in a row. The 2010 mobile data traffic growth rate was higher than anticipated. Last year's mobile data traffic was three times the size of the entire global Internet in 2000. Global mobile data traffic in 2010 was over three times greater than the total global Internet traffic in 2000. Mobile video traffic is manifesting exponential growth. It will exceed 50% for the first time in 2011. Mobile video traffic was 49.8% of total mobile data traffic at the end of 2010, and Cisco VNI forecasts it will account for 52.8% of traffic by the end of 2011. Projections are for global mobile data traffic to increase an astounding 26-fold between 2010 and 2015. Mobile data traffic will grow at a compound annual growth rate (CAGR) of 92% from 2010 to 2015.

Another area within technology that will see increasing growth is video streaming. Two-thirds of the world's mobile data traffic will be video by 2015. Mobile video will more than double every year between 2010 and 2015. Mobile video has the strongest growth rate of any application category measured within the 2011 Cisco VNI forecast at this time. The mobile-only

Internet population will grow 56-fold from 14 million at the end of 2010 to 788 million by the end of 2015.

Government Spending

Funding within the industry soon will be not only from the private sector but from national governments, which are initiating large projects and even their own national entities to build out broadband solutions for citizens. For example, Australia has embarked on an enormous high-end broadband build-out throughout that roomy homeland. This was first announced in April 2009. The Australian government established a new company to design, build, and operate a new high-speed network, to be known as the National Broadband Network (NBN). The NBN overnight became the single largest infrastructure investment made by an Australian government in that nation's history. In June 2011, NBN and private firm Telstra announced that they had entered into definitive agreements on the rollout of the NBN. Construction of the network is planned to begin in late 2011, delivering its first services in 2012, and to be completed by 2015. The spending is enormous. The network is estimated to cost A\$35.9 billion to build over a 10-year period, including an Australian investment of A\$27.5 billion.

The United Kingdom's government announced in 2010 that every community in the UK will gain access to super-fast broadband by 2015. The government has earmarked £830m for the scheme as a result of a study by regulator Ofcom that revealed that fewer than 1% of UK homes have a super-fast broadband connection. China in April approved a stimulus plan, calling for $22 billion investment in fiber networks that will establish more than 80 million fiber broadband ports by the end of 2012. China Telecom is going to triple the user numbers of its new high-speed optical fiber broadband by the end of 2011 to 30 million and expects to swell that number to more than 100 million by the end of China's 12th five-year plan (2011–2015). This five-year plan, supported financially by the Chinese government, would maintain a total investment in infrastructure reaching 2 trillion yuan ($303 billion). All these government projects are advancing despite the poor economic environment and will no doubt drive industry spending in the next decade.

Strong Financial Characteristics

A strong financial position is always important to a technology firm. Large technology firms such as Microsoft, Oracle, and Cisco Systems maintain high cash levels, high return on equity, and significant operating margins. In today's technology environment, firms with a strong balance sheet are best positioned to commit high levels of investment in research and development and maintain the funding necessary to garner government contracts. Firms today are not competing just with other private firms but with government-backed entities that have nearly unlimited financing. Only those technology firms with the highest resources will be best positioned for the rapid growth within broadband over the next decade. The technology sector has a plethora of firms with rock-solid balance sheets and high amounts of cash. With an incredible $76.1 billion in cash stacked on its balance sheet as of July 2011, Apple's cash hoard exceeds the gross domestic products of 126 of the world's 195 countries. Microsoft has well over $50 billion cash, and software giant Oracle maintains nearly $30 billion. This list of firms within the sector with high percentage weights of cash is quite long. The sector is thus well positioned from a balance sheet perspective to maintain growth either organically or through acquisitions through the next decade.

Sub-Sector Analysis

The Computer Hardware and Equipment Industry

The computer hardware and equipment industry designs, manufactures, services, and supports a wide range of computer systems, notebooks, netbooks, tablets, smartphones, and servers. Over the past decade, investors have favored a few relatively large-cap companies, including Apple, Dell, Cisco, IBM, Hitachi, and Hewlett-Packard. In the hardware space, the continued decline in average selling prices (ASPs) in the personal computer market has been a significant challenge for companies that focus strictly on computer sales.

In the computer hardware industry, software has always driven hardware sales. Unfortunately, the market has not seen a significant personal computer application since Windows 95. Most of the new software platforms built today are for the mobile computing industry (i.e., for smartphones and tablet computers). Although the Internet remains the overriding force behind personal computer sales, the rise of wireless technologies and the subsequent convergence of devices such as cell phones with personal computers is providing a new spark for the companies within this sector. The storage industry market is also part of this industry and is led by EMC. This specialty industry is composed of companies that manufacture and/or distribute products considered as add-ons to (or even basic components of) computers, (e.g., storage devices). Today's computers need a lot of data storage capacity in order to use more sophisticated software and operate in more complex multi-user environments. In fact, the amount of storage capacity being used is expected to surge exponentially over the next several years, driven in large part by video and the Internet. Almost every technology development today is leading to increased demand for storage.

One of the innovative trends within storage is cloud computing. Cloud computing differs from the typical server model by providing applications away from a server. Storage capability is provided and managed through the user's own web browser. This removes the necessity for version upgrades or license management on an individual client's computing software. It also allows offsite storage of information, critical for easy access and encryption. According to data compiled by the research firm IDC, the global revenue for servers deployed in public and private clouds is expected to approach $9.4 billion by 2015. This revenue will mainly be driven by firm technology managers. IDC further estimates that the number of servers shipped for operation in public clouds will have a compound annual growth rate (CAGR) of 21%.

On the mobile hardware front, it is becoming increasingly apparent that a more portable system of computing is here to stay. Although the time-honored desktop system will be with us for years to come, the race to the emerging markets will be done through more mobile computing systems. Clearly, fewer people are buying new personal computers today because of market saturation and the rise of new entrants such as Apple's iPad and RIMM's playbook. Of course, the personal computer is still alive and kicking, given that more than one million personal computers are sold every day. But sales have slowed in recent years. The U.S. and European markets have fared the worst, suffering this decade from declines compared with previous years. Market research firms IDC and Gartner, Inc. indicated that personal computer shipments worldwide grew at just over 2% in the second quarter of 2011, short of both firms' expectations.

One of the most urgent concerns for hardware companies is that the personal computer has become ubiquitous in many markets. That has presented the industry with a classic business problem: how to find new ways to sell a conventional product. Personal computer sales are decelerating in the United States because the same technological advances that fueled the personal computer industry's ascension—faster processors and lower costs every few years—are now benefiting the mobile devices that are seizing the momentum. Consumers can now use smaller gadgets to do many of the same things they once did with personal computers, such as surfing the Internet, storing photos, watching videos, and sending e-mail. Apple even boasts that its customers can edit movies on their iPhones.

Consumers' increasing demand for tablets is a looming threat to the personal computer producers as well. Some 50 million tablets are expected to be sold worldwide this year, and that could double to as many as 100 million next year, according to the IDC. Although that is still tiny compared with sales of 362 million personal computers this year, as estimated by IDC, the personal computer industry has reason to agonize because of how quickly the tablet has been able to claim such a hefty share of the market. Forrester Research has predicted tablet sales in the U.S. will overtake netbook sales by 2012 and desktop sales by 2015. The companies that are best positioned to take advantage of the trend towards smartphones and tablets will be the decade's biggest winners (see Table 6.1).

TABLE 6.1 Major Hardware and Equipment Companies

	Industry	Market Cap
Apple, Inc.	Hardware and Equipment	363,252.75
IBM	Hardware and Equipment	217,119.78
Cisco Systems, Inc.	Hardware and Equipment	88,057.96
Hewlett-Packard Co.	Hardware and Equipment	75,146.66
EMC Corp.	Hardware and Equipment	54,710.73
Ericsson Telephone Co.	Hardware and Equipment	40,286.85
Dell, Inc.	Hardware and Equipment	31,251.53
Sony Corp.	Hardware and Equipment	25,196.29
Panasonic Corp.	Hardware and Equipment	24,408.76
Nokia Corp.	Hardware and Equipment	21,383.70
Neap, Inc.	Hardware and Equipment	17,780.00
Motorola Solutions, Inc.	Hardware and Equipment	15,744.00
Research in Motion, Ltd.	Hardware and Equipment	13,344.05

Source: Standard & Poor's.

The Computer Software Industry

The computer software industry is characterized by significant expenses for up-front development, marketing, and technical support for initial versions of software products. Software companies are divided into major categories including word processing, data base, graphics, and Internet security. Major players include Microsoft, SAP, Oracle, and Symantec. Gross margins in the software business are often 70 to 80% because there is very little expense needed to support a software company. The software industry continues to grow at a rapid pace. DataMonitor has forecast that in 2013 the global software market will have a value around $457 billion, which would be an increase of around 50% from 2008's revenue. Software companies today are extremely well capitalized and were able to stash away a significant amount of cash during the downturn. At the end of 2010, cash accounted for nearly a quarter of firm's value within the software index, as compared with 7% of total assets for all U.S. companies. The top 10 technology companies added more than $26 billion in cash to their balance sheets in 2010, and they presently hold a collective $227 billion in cash. With such a high percentage of cash, software industry mergers and acquisitions continued at a rapid pace. Activity in the United States remained healthy in the first half of 2011, with 500 announced transactions overall.

One characteristic of the software industry is the high cost of labor. Labor is the largest expense item since software development often involves working in teams of 6, 12, or even 100 people. Furthermore, software projects often involve long lead times between diverse versions. Software publishers write application software for a specific operating system. This creates a standardized format and ensures programs will work with one another easily and without problems. The newest trend in the software industry is to sell software as a subscription instead of in a shrink-wrapped package. This ensures continuity of

TABLE 6.2 Major Software Companies

	Industry	Market Cap
Microsoft Corp.	Software	233,756.31
Oracle Corp.	Software	155,334.02
Sap AG	Software	76,724.57
VMware, Inc.	Software	42,578.25
Salesforce.com, Inc.	Software	19,562.79
Intuit, Inc.	Software	14,336.66
Symantec	Software	14,725.50
Adobe Systems, Inc.	Software	13,838.14
Citrix Systems, Inc.	Software	13,689.83
Check Point Software Technologies, Ltd.	Software	12,079.72
CA, Inc.	Software	11,264.82
Dassault Systemes SA	Software	10,634.80
Red Hat, Inc.	Software	8,234.34
Autodesk, Inc.	Software	7,930.97
BMC Software, Inc.	Software	7,889.64

Source: Standard & Poor's.

revenue and lessens the wild swings in earnings that typically impact software firms (see Table 6.2).

The Semiconductor Industry

The semiconductor industry designs, manufactures, and sells computer components such as microprocessors, chipsets, flash memory products, graphics products, network and communications products, systems management software, and digital imaging products. The semiconductor industry serves as an enabler and marker of technological advancement. Developments in the industry determine the way people work, entertain, and communicate among each other. Semiconductors are used in a multitude of ways, including as control systems in cars, cell phones, computers, and MP3 players. Semiconductors are made of silicon, which is economical to extract from sand. During the past decade immense changes have occurred within the industry, with a large amount of semiconductor firms streamlining operations, reducing costs, and transferring additional production to lower-cost countries. This movement has led to the expansion of the Asian semiconductor production market, where the greater part of memory production and backend operations have shifted. According to Gartner, overall industry revenue is expected to grow about 4.6% in 2011. Gartner projected the industry for the first time will pass the $300 billion mark by the end of that year. The most up-to-date research report from IHS iSuppli calculated that by 2015 the global semiconductor industry will hit a new milestone and the overall revenues will be more than $400 billion. IHS projected the fastest growth within the industry will be in image sensors, NAND flash memory, LED sensors, and PLD chips.

With the greater need for bandwidth, build-out of networking infrastructure, the propagation of the Internet, and the growth of wireless communication, the semiconductor industry will continue to have strong demand. There are a variety of major players, each generally specializing in a niche market. Intel leads sales of microprocessors. Advanced Micro Devices ranks number two in this arena. Texas Instruments is the most widely diversified firm within the industry. Qualcomm, Maxim Integrated, Analog Devices, ST Microelectronics, and Xilinx are additional major players (see Table 6.3).

The Internet Industry

The Internet industry is characterized by rapid development of content over computer networks. The Internet industry encompasses all companies engaged in creating, developing, or processing electronic information through computer network systems. The hurried pace of growth in the Internet has resulted

TABLE 6.3 Major Semiconductor Companies

	Industry	Market Cap
Intel Corp.	Semiconductors	119,560.10
Qualcomm	Semiconductors	92,368.86
Taiwan Semiconductor Manufacturing	Semiconductors	63,800.74
Texas Instruments, Inc.	Semiconductors	34,974.40
Broadcom Corp.	Semiconductors	19,709.40
ASML Holding NV	Semiconductor Equipment and Materials	15,599.47
Altera Corp.	Semiconductors	13,164.15
ARM Holdings PLC	Semiconductors	12,670.71
Infineon Technologies AG	Semiconductors	10,726.14
Analog Devices, Inc.	Semiconductors	10,394.29
SanDisk Corp.	Semiconductor Memory	10,071.39
Marvell Technology Group, Ltd.	Semiconductors	9,158.77
Xilinx, Inc	Semiconductors	8,526.58
NVIDIA Corp.	Semiconductors	8,301.99
Micron Technology, Inc.	Semiconductor Memory	7,449.54

Source: Standard & Poor's.

in intense competition for web audience attention and users of
Internet software. Many of these companies are a direct out-
growth of the computer software industry. Major players include
Google, Baidu, Yahoo, and eBay. Since the beginning of the Internet wave in 1998, many Internet companies have gone out of
business. The reason for their collapse has been very fundamental. First, many failed Internet companies lacked the resources
necessary to fund business and expansion from existing operations. Second, there were serious questions about business models. Stock valuation based on price/earnings or price/book ratios
reached stratospheric levels during the Internet boom of the late
1990s. These frothy valuations were unsustainable. After the

Internet bust of the early 2000s, investors did not want to continue to finance a company with an unproven concept, even if it meant passing up a ground-floor opportunity to prosper.

Since 2000, there has been an industry shakeout that put many Internet companies out of business. After a decade of industry consolidation, choosing industry winners today is not difficult. Companies such as Google and eBay have carved out lucrative niches within the industry. However, the industry is constantly evolving with new entrants proliferating. These include LinkedIn, which recently went public, and numerous other firms such as Facebook and Groupon, which will both soon become public companies. Growth is still far above that of other industries. Deutsche Bank research expects online advertising in the U.S. to reach $28.5 billion in 2011, representing a healthy 15% growth year over year. In Cisco System's 2011 report, the firm predicted that the total amount of global Internet traffic will quadruple between 2010 and 2015. Cisco's report projected the increase in Internet traffic between 2014 and 2015 alone will be 200 exabytes, which is greater than the total amount of Internet traffic generated globally in 2010. Factors seem to suggest that companies with a strong content platform, excellent financing capabilities, and strong distribution strategies will continue to be the winners as the market continues to evolve over the next decade (see Table 6.4).

TABLE 6.4 Major Internet Companies

	Industry	Market Cap
Google, Inc.	Internet	197,265.05
Baidu, Inc.	Internet	55,250.96
Yahoo, Inc.	Internet	17,589.71
LinkedIn Corp.	Internet	9,509.40
SINA Corp.	Internet	6,859.46
NetEase.com, Inc.	Internet	6,560.67

Source: Standard & Poor's.

Investing in the Technology Sector

The technology sector should account for 5 to 7.5% of your stock portfolio. This sector provides the highest possible investment return in any given year. However, it is also a high-risk sector, alongside financials. The technology sector suffered dramatically during 2000–2002 period. This substantially lowered the sector's long-term investment returns. Because technology stocks are so volatile and the opportunity for loss is high, a diversified strategy should be followed. Stock selection within technology should cover a broad range of the four sub-sectors.

Three to six stocks should be chosen from the list of companies above. Special focus should be on industry leaders. The quickest way to lose money in this sector is to focus on the laggards. In choosing an individual stock from the technology list, consider the following guidelines:

- Choose only firms that are No. 1 or No. 2 in their respective industries (or in a particular market segment) and maintain low betas.
- Choose companies that have or are developing products or services that represent significant technological advancements or improvements.
- Select those that have strong fundamentals, strong management, and strong product positioning.
- Broadly diversify among the various sub-sectors. Do not concentrate your investment in any one sub-sector.
- Select companies of a large size (5 billion market cap >).
- Attempt to add to your portfolio when technology stocks are out of favor (see case studies).
- Stay defensive; never get too excited about this sector. Keep your investments within tight boundaries.

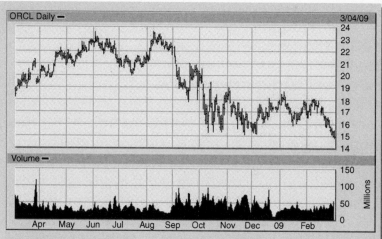

FIGURE 6.1 Case Study No. 7: Oracle, March 2009
Source: Charts provided by Commodity Systems, Inc. (CSI) 2012.

At one time in early 2000, Oracle traded at $40 a share. At that level, it was priced at a ridiculous 60 times earnings (P/E). By early 2009, the stock price of Oracle had collapsed to $14 a share. After years of unfavorable performance, Oracle finally offered an attractive entry point for astute technology investors. I first examined Oracle's financials starting with my favored ratios (see Table 6.5).

TABLE 6.5 Oracle Ratios

2008 E.P.S.	$1.30
Current Ratio	1.8
Debt/Equity	22%
Interest Cover	12
Operating Margin	40%
R.O.E.	26%
Price/Earnings	10.6
FCF Yield	9.8%

Source: Standard & Poor's.

(*continued*)

(continued)

- Oracle was by far the leader within the software industry.
- Oracle had outstanding liquidity ratios and a very small amount of debt.
- Despite the technology sector crash during the financial meltdown of 2008, operating margins actually rose during the previous five years, rising to 47.4% from 40.6%. The margins were far and above the best within Oracle's industry.
- Oracle further reaffirmed its expectation to increase its market share through the recession. With SAP, Oracle was becoming a dominant company within application and database software.
- Oracle's P/E ratio of 10 was the lowest in 15 years, and its historical P/E ratio range was from 10 to 85 over the preceding two decades.
- Our expected 5-year growth rate in earnings for Oracle was 15%. The PEG ratio was 0.8, extremely low for a premier technology company.
- Oracle also met our criteria for FCF (free cash flow) yield, at nearly 10%.

I purchased Oracle in March of 2009 at an initial price of $15.35. My original target price for Oracle was set at $25. Oracle was one of the better performing technology stocks during 2009 due to the company's stellar balance sheet and consistent revenue stream. I continued to hold Oracle for my clients through 2011. My expectation for Oracle's earnings per share in 2011 was $2.20, double the amount earned in 2007. My price target was set at $40 a share by the end of 2012.

(continued)

FIGURE 6.2 Case Study No. 8: Broadcom, June 2011
Source: Charts provided by Commodity Systems, Inc. (2012).

During the first half of 2011, the SPDR S&P Semiconductor ETF had dropped in price from $64 a share to $52. The semiconductor industry was under pressure from weakening U.S. economic growth along with concerns over the debt crisis in Greece and in the United States. I initiated the process of breaking down the industry, looking for leaders within the space that were under price pressure. Broadcom was a semiconductor company that focused on several growth-end markets, including networking, broadband, and mobile devices. This included smartphones and the new tablet computers. I inspected Broadcom's financials starting with my favored ratios in Table 6.6.

- Broadcom was positioned well within the industry with its focus on chips for the highest growth areas, including cell phones (with Apple) and tablets.
- Broadcom's diverse portfolio of semiconductor chips makes its revenue base less unpredictable than many of

(*continued*)

(continued)

TABLE 6.6 Broadcom Ratios

2011 E.P.S.	$1.95
Debt/Equity	11%
Interest Cover	15.3
Operating Margin	17%
R.O.A.	12%
Price/Earnings	15.5
Price/Sales	2.5
FCF Yield	7.4%

Source: Standard & Poor's.

its competitors. The company acquired a 4G chip-making startup, Beceem, in 2011 to further diversify its lineup and to fill in a missing link in its product array.

- Broadcom had a very low debt ratio of 11% and had $3.8 billion of cash on its balance sheet. Broadcom's operating margins had advanced from less than 5% in 2007 to 17% by 2011.
- Broadcom traded at a low price/sales ratio of only 2.5. During the past decade, Broadcom had traded at a range of 1.7 to 7.5. With higher operating margins, profits, and lower debt, Broadcom should be trading at a much higher price/sales ratio of 5. Taking five times expected 2012 sales of 14.3 would gave me a price target of $71.50.

I purchased Broadcom during June 2011 at an initial price of $32.85.

CHAPTER 7

The Financial Sector

I'd like to live like a poor man with lots of money.

Pablo Picasso

The financial services industry is an important facilitator of economic activity. The primary function of any financial institution is to expedite the exchange of financial resources between savers and borrowers. The financial services sector includes five sub-sectors: banks, insurance companies, consumer financial services, securities companies, and S&Ls. Overall, the financial sector includes more than 5,400 stocks. The sector represents 14.8% of the market capitalization of the S&P 500, making it the third largest sector of the index. As a result of the financial crisis of 2008, the sector lost much of its luster. At one point in 2006, the sector accounted for over 21% of the S&P 500.

Despite the poor performance in the sector in the most recent bear market, the category's returns are still above average and are impressive for the long term. For the 24-year period ending December 31, 2010, the sector generated a 9.51% annualized return. Remarkably, a substantial proportion of the category's long-term gains have come not from small, high-risk companies, but from established, highly visible, and financially sound firms such as Wells Fargo, Goldman Sachs, and Chubb.

Sectoral Factors

I believe there are three distinctive characteristics that favor owning financial firms:

- Global demographic changes
- Globalization trends
- Continued low interest rates

The combination of these factors should enable financial stocks to generate the earnings that make these holdings very attractive for long-term investors.

Demographics

Data from the U.S. Census Bureau indicate that the number of Americans in the 45-to-64 age group is estimated to increase nearly 47% from 2005 to 2015. It is expected that during the next 10 years, a U.S. citizen has turned 50 once every eight seconds. Concerned about the reliability of Social Security, people in this group are just now taking control of their financial futures. The vast majority are approaching their 50s and will have an increasing need for financial and retirement services from annuities to tax planning to investment management services. Baby boomers have historically undersaved for retirement. In recent years much has been made about how the savings rate in this country was hovering around (or even below) zero. More and more over the preceding decade, Americans were living beyond their means via credit. With some banks reeling from extending credit to people they should not have, some economic pundits have been predicting an increase in the domestic savings rate for years. The increase in the savings rate could have a dramatic impact not only on the economy but on the financial services firms that manage this country's wealth. If the savings rate returned to just half its level in 1992, it would reach 4% of disposable income, up from 0.6% at present. Each percent increase in the U.S. savings rate amounts to nearly $100 billion of annual savings. The savings rate surged to 6.9% during 2010, the highest level since the early 1990s. Financial firms should benefit heavily from this new savings trend over the ensuing decade as they gather additional assets and charge fees.

Globalization

The continued development of foreign economies will spur demand for investment, insurance, and banking services. Global financial institutions that anticipate the impending boom will be the best prepared for this tremendous opportunity over the next 10 years. The marketplaces in Europe, Japan, and in key economies elsewhere will be prime targets of business expansion. Alliances and partnerships between trusted brands will be extremely powerful. In addition, mergers will continue to accelerate as financial firms looking to gain exposure to these markets make unsolicited bids. With the higher cost of government regulation, the global financial markets will continue to be dominated by a relatively few large multinational financial companies capable of attaining enormous economies of scale, while offering a broad portfolio of products to service the growing demands of their client base.

Low Interest Rates

The financial services sector's high investment return has been aided in no small part by a long-term decline in interest rates from their highs in 1981. Lower rates have generally meant lower funding costs for banking and investment institutions. They have also encouraged investors to search the stock and bond markets for alternatives to lower-yielding traditional savings accounts. Although the decline in rates is most likely over, interest rates are expected to remain stable over the next several years as our economy exits the deep recession of 2008. Interest rates in particular tend to play a leading role in determining the short-term price movements of financial stocks. Higher interest costs can have a wide ranging impact on banks' profitability. First, rising interest rates slow down economic growth, reducing demand for financial services such as loans. Higher rates can also lead to higher loan defaults, with corresponding damage to a lender's bottom line. Interest income has always been a large portion of revenue for many financial companies; thus, interest-rate changes can flow directly to the bottom line.

Although many pundits are resigned to the fact that higher interest rates are coming, the substantiation is lacking. The 1920s, the late 1980s, and the Japanese real estate bubble of the early 1990s constitute the three great real estate events of the last 100 years. In two of the cases, the 1920s and Japan's 1990s, a debt bubble had been built up over the previous decade. In each case, interest rates remained extremely low for decades as economic growth was stunted by the high level of total consumer and government debt. Logic holds that in the decade of the 2010s, the U.S. economy will most likely suffer the same uncertain outlook, and interest rates thus would remain below historical averages.

Sub-Sector Analysis

The Banking Industry

The banking industry represents nearly 20% of the S&P financial services index. The banking industry has historically been one of the most heavily regulated industries in the United States. This was a direct result of the 1929 stock market crash, which resulted in hundreds of bank failures. Banks are the spine of the global economy, providing capital for modernization, infrastructure, job creation, and overall affluence. Banks also play a vital role in society, affecting not only spending by individual consumers but the development of entire industries.

According to the FDIC, the United States has the largest banking system in the world, consisting of 7,830 banks with total assets of $13.22 trillion as of 2010. Major firms within the industry include JP Morgan Chase, Bank of America, Wells Fargo, and PNC Bank. These banks, bruised in financial calamity of 2008 and 2009, are still among the best positioned in regard to capital and revenue trends. With noteworthy raises in capital completed during the past two years, the balance sheets and income statements of the largest U.S. banks have finally stabilized. But there are tremendous headwinds facing the industry over the next decade. This includes fragile loan growth trends, higher expenses, higher Tier 1 capital ratio requirements, and fee-reduction pressure from regulators. The banking industry's profits are continuing to be compressed as a result of this higher regulation and enforcement, most remarkably in the credit and debit card space. Future squeezes on profitability will continue as the increased capital standards from the Basel III Accord and other Financial Stability Oversight Council (FSOC) determinations take effect.

In July 2010, President Obama signed into law the Wall Street Reform and Consumer Protection Act, often referred to as the Dodd–Frank Act. This far-reaching legislation contains an immense amount of provisions affecting the banking industry. The Act also created a new Consumer Financial Protection Bureau (CFPB) with rule-making, enforcement, and investigative authority over consumer financial protection statutes. The CFPB is authorized to be the principal rulemaker on these laws, and the regulators, in turn, are authorized to enforce rules prescribed by the CFPB. The new CFPB regulations will heighten the cost of doing business for banks. The Act further directs the Federal Reserve to set interchange rates in electronic debit card transactions involving issuers with more than $10 billion in assets. The Federal Reserve is directed to regulate the "reasonableness" of the fees. There are many other regulations as part of the Act that are coming. The leisurely progress made on finalizing rules has made banks wary. Of the 400 new rules due from the regulators, only 12% have been finalized while 33% have missed the time perimeter set for completion.

Despite this enhanced government regulatory burden, the banking sector is continuing to return to well-being and is now looking outside the box to find new ways to make profits. Today, banks are implementing important modifications to the business models, all of which will ultimately increase costs for consumers. These alterations include higher fees on checking accounts and limitations on debit card use. The cancellation of rewards programs is also being implemented. All of these regulations have driven return on equity and net interest margin lower for most of the major U.S. banking institutions. For example, the FDIC announced that eight of the 10 largest banks in the United States—which together control more than half of all loans in the country—showed a decline in net interest margin during the first half of 2011. During the first quarter of 2011, the value of loans outstanding held by banks declined by nearly $127 billion. Banks are now searching for any alternative to return to higher revenue and profitability, including opening up smaller "lite-branches" (i.e., ATM-only locations) and reducing workforce at many branch locations (see Table 7.1).

The Securities Industry

The securities industry accounts for roughly 25% of the benchmark. Major securities firms include Morgan Stanley, Goldman Sachs, and Nomura. Merrill Lynch is no longer part of the index

TABLE 7.1 Major Banking Companies

	Industry	Market Cap
JPMorgan Chase & Co.	Banking	160,735.55
Wells Fargo & Co.	Banking	147,777.43
Citigroup, Inc	Banking	111,977.49
Bank of America Corp.	Banking	98,391.07
UBS AG	Banking	63,151.42
U.S. Bancorp	Banking	50,208.50
Deutsche Bank AG	Banking	50,072.17
Banco Bilbao Vizcaya Argentaria SA	Banking	46,795.26
Barclays PLC	Banking	44,342.26
Credit Suisse Group	Banking	43,163.94
PNC Financial Services Group, Inc.	Banking	28,571.90
BB&T Corp.	Banking	17,885.28
SunTrust Banks, Inc.	Banking	13,148.41
Fifth Third Bancorp	Banking	11,621.91
M&T Bank Corp.	Banking	10,416.86

Source: Standard & Poor's.

following its acquisition by Bank of America. The securities industry is extremely vulnerable to wide swings in economic activity. During recessions, securities firms often lay off personnel because of a reduction in activity with declining new initial public offerings (IPOs), fewer mergers and acquisitions (M&A), and reductions in stock-trading activity. The opposite occurs in boom times as the industry is marked by substantial volumes in stock-trading activity, which increases demand for additional IPOs and M&A.

Securities firms contribute to capital raising by assisting corporations and others in their efforts to issue debt and equity securities, and by selling these newly created securities to individuals and institutions. The major old-line investment firms have been under fire as the result of the gradual shift from full-service to discount brokerage houses. Discount brokers execute

TABLE 7.2 Major Securities Companies

	Industry	Market Cap
The Goldman Sachs Group, Inc.	Securities	69,878.73
Morgan Stanley	Securities	34,368.64
The Charles Schwab Corp.	Securities	18,016.47
Nomura Holdings, Inc.	Securities	17,464.30
TD Ameritrade Holding Corp.	Securities	10,490.18

Source: Standard & Poor's.

orders at low prices and have increased their market share to nearly 20% of retail commission revenue. Public company discounters include Charles Schwab, Ameritrade Securities, and the smaller E*Trade Group. These relatively newer securities firms have yet to enter the highly profitable IPO market, a potential risk to the established old-line players. Securities firms are the most volatile section of the financial industry. These stocks generally move up and down with the stock market to a much greater degree. Investors should be vigilant as to the timing of investing in this sector (see Table 7.2).

The Asset Management Industry

The asset management industry, also known as the investment management industry, is one of the largest global industries. This industry handles transactions worth trillions of dollars annually, and it makes up a significant segment of the financial sector throughout the world. This industry manages huge amounts of investments and helps clients reach their financial goals. With the growing complexity in financial markets, investors are demanding more service and better analysis than ever.

For asset management firms, the extraordinary demographic shift of baby boomers will bring with it some decisive implications. According to consulting firm McKinsey & Company, investable assets controlled by retirees and near-retirees will swell to almost two-thirds of all assets by 2012. This group of investors will demand alternatives to what has been sold over the previous two decades. Retirees are more concerned with securing pension-type products such as annuities. The traditional model of accumulation will be less relevant to the profitability of these firms in the next several years. Asset management firms that have products to meet these needs will be best positioned. This also means that asset management companies will be competing more with traditional insurance companies for new clients.

For asset management firms, the recent financial crisis resulted in poor investment performance, which led to declining assets under management and reduced fees. The reality of diminishing assets and resources has led to decreased profitability since the golden days of the 1990s. Asset management companies are now appraising their infrastructure costs; they are deciding whether to chase important in-house development or to choose outsourcing. Many are choosing the latter, as outsourcing allows firms to control costs and still maintain consistent, high-quality management of portfolios. As with the banking sector, regulation will play a large part in the future profitability of the industry. The Dodd–Frank legislation contains new requirements that may have a collateral impact on asset management firms, including requirements related to incentive compensation, asset-backed securities, and financial incentives for whistleblowers. The Act also provides for a budding new standard of care for broker-dealers and the possibility of a changed regulatory oversight configuration (see Table 7.3).

The Insurance Industry

The insurance industry (including accident and health, life, property–casualty and multi-line insurance, insurance brokers, and specialty insurers) constitutes roughly 19% of the benchmark. The insurance industry has undergone a profound change

TABLE 7.3 Major Asset Management Companies

	Industry	Market Cap
BlackRock. Inc.	Asset Management	34,316.78
Bank of New York Mellon	Asset Management	31,179.69
Franklin Resources	Asset Management	28,167.17
State Street Corp.	Asset Management	20,902.48
T. Rowe Price Group	Asset Management	14,561.75
Northern Trust Corp.	Asset Management	10,858.17
Invesco, Ltd.	Asset Management	10,248.77

Source: Standard & Poor's.

in its business model. Over the past quarter of a century, insurers such as AIG and Metlife have seen their business shift from basic life and property insurance coverage to more complex under-writing. This includes providing insurance not just to consumers but to other complex entities such pension and hedge funds. On the individual side, the advent and growth of annuity products has altered the landscape. This has fundamentally changed the way insurance firms do business, as they now concentrate on managing investment risk rather than simply the mortality risk of an individual.

As a result, insurance firms now compete more directly with financial services firms. Some insurance companies have even shifted their product mix to offer consumer finance and credit cards. Homeowner and auto insurance is the most important area of the property and casualty insurance business. Competition is often based on price. Property and casualty (P&C) insurers have tended to stay within their niche. The greatest potential threat may be the entry of banks into the P&C insurance business. Overall, the insurance industry is less affected by interest rates than banks and thrifts. These companies generally offer defensive characteristics during economic slowdowns. Therefore, investor exposure in this area offers an excellent diversification benefit.

Insurance companies today are looking to expand globally more than ever before. The judgment is hard to counter; growth in the North American and European insurance markets is slowing rapidly, and emerging countries with a growing middle class and relatively higher GDP growth offer the potential for expanding sales. In the older-line markets such as the United States, the prospect of baby boomers drawing down trillions in retirement assets offers insurance companies an exceptional opportunity to take market share from asset management firms. But insurers need to move aggressively because asset management firms are creating new products to take advantage of this trend (see Table 7.4).

TABLE 7.4 **Major Insurance Companies**

	Industry	Market Cap
Berkshire Hathaway, Inc.	Insurance	173,954.83
MetLife, Inc.	Insurance	43,560.64
AXA SA	Insurance	42,906.39
ING Groep N.V.	Insurance	41,150.96
Prudential PLC	Insurance	28,687.30
Prudential Financial, Inc.	Insurance	28,635.84
Manulife Financial Corp.	Insurance	28,408.31
The Travelers Companies, Inc.	Insurance	23,085.07
ACE, Ltd.	Insurance	22,599.20
Aflac, Inc.	Insurance	21,542.48
Chubb Corp	Insurance	18,278.23
Marsh & McLennan Companies, Inc.	Insurance	16,174.73
Sun Life Financial, Inc.	Insurance	16,077.23
Aon Corp.	Insurance	15,905.63
The Allstate Corp.	Insurance	14,496.48
Progressive Corp.	Insurance	12,904.97
Hartford Financial Services Group, Inc.	Insurance	10,428.31

Source: Standard & Poor's.

The Credit Card Servicing Industry

The credit services companies have traditionally offered credit card services to the average consumer. However, in recent years, many credit services companies have branched out into other credit areas such as boat and motor home loans. The use of credit cards has grown considerably; during the past decade, the credit card interchange fees collected by American Express, Visa, and MasterCard have risen from 16.6 billion in 2001 to 65 billion in 2010. The credit card system is beneficial for consumers. It reduces the need to carry cash and lessens the trouble of storing outsized amounts of cash in brick and mortar locations for merchants. The reality of interchange fees mean that ultimately merchandise must be marked up by all vendors to compensate for the costs of paying the credit card companies. The credit card habit is growing as more consumers transfer from cash to credit for their everyday needs. Its commonness is further strengthened by the increasing prevalence of Ecommerce on the web. The industry is a more volatile one, strongly influenced by the general economy, which if weak, heavily influences overall spending and fees. It is important to point out that several of the strongest competitors in the financing business are units of larger companies in other industries, such as GE Capital Services, Ford Motor Credit, and GMAC, and are not technically part of the financial sector.

Regulation for the industry has been as noteworthy as the Dodd–Frank Act was to the banking industry. The Credit Card Accountability Responsibility and Disclosure Act was passed in May 2009. It is a very comprehensive credit card reform legislation that aimed to establish fair and transparent practices relating to the extension of credit. The Act has also had a major impact on the industry. In mid-2011, The Consumer Financial Protection Bureau released data showing that credit card late fees dropped from $901 million in January 2010 to $427 million in

TABLE 7.5 Major Credit Card Service Companies

	Industry	Market Cap
Visa, Inc.	Credit Services	71,004.31
MasterCard, Inc.	Credit Services	38,585.65
Capital One Financial Corp.	Credit Services	21,947.13
Discover Financial Services	Credit Services	13,974.60

Source: Standard & Poor's.

November 2010, due to a cap of $25 on the first late fee on an account and $35 for a second late fee within six months of the first offense. One of the major provisions of the Act was the imposition of new rules that prevented credit card issuers from penalizing cardholders for going over the card's limit amount, unless the cardholder desired that these charges be established. As a result of this alteration, many credit card issuers eradicated over-the-limit fees. These fees were as high as $39 before the new rules were put in place. A major negative for consumers of the Act was that credit card interest rates had risen from 13.26% to 14.27%, making it more difficult to find a card with a low interest rate today. Overall, the Act seems to have achieved the goals set out by the government. Credit card service firms will have to look for new methods of improving revenue and profitability in the coming years (see Table 7.5).

The Thrift Industry

The thrift or S&L industry now represents less than 2% of the financial company universe and consists of only a handful of smaller companies. Thrifts derive their revenue primarily from home mortgages. Thrifts have been one of the most volatile industries within the financial sector. Washington Mutual was the largest single entity in the industry and is no longer a stand-alone firm. Thrifts thus have far more sensitivity than banks to economic factors such as consumer defaults and/or rising interest rates.

Investing in the Financial Sector

The financial sector should be the smallest exposure of any sector, from a 2.5 to 5% segment in your overall portfolio. The sector provides an excellent low cross-correlation with other sectors despite the lowest overall return. Selection within financials should cover the broad range of sub-sectors previously listed. Three to six stocks should be chosen from this list. In choosing an individual stock from the financials list, consider the following:

- Broadly diversify among the various sub-sectors. Any concentration should be on the largest and best-capitalized banks.
- Select companies of a large size (5 billion market cap >).
- Seek out firms with low volatility or beta to further reduce the risk component of the sector.
- Favor industry leaders within each sub-sector.
- Attempt to add to your portfolio sub-sectors that are out of favor (see Chapter 11).
- When the Federal Reserve starts raising interest rates, reduce exposure to financials. Especially avoid thrifts and brokers. Concentrate your investments on more defensive financials (e.g., insurers).

Franklin Resources is one of the largest asset management firms in the world serving both individual and institutional investors. The firm's well-known products include mutual funds that are marketed under the names of Franklin, Templeton, and Mutual Series. Before the financial collapse of 2008, Franklin Resources traded at a high price of $142 a

(continued)

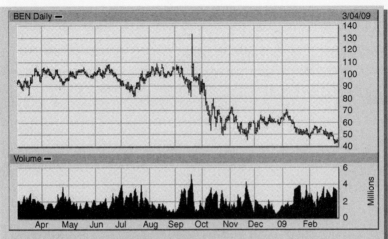

FIGURE 7.1 Case Study No. 9: Franklin Resources, February 2009
Source: Charts provided by Commodity Systems, Inc. (CSI) 2012.

share. As the stock market collapsed, the shares of this asset management company fell precipitously to less than $50 a share. We had positioned our portfolios with a higher percentage of health care during 2007 as we felt the economy was slowing dramatically. During early 2009, we started rotating out of the more defensive and health care sectors and into firms that would benefit in an eventual economic recovery. Franklin Resources fit our profile, with a leadership position within the asset management industry, a strong balance sheet, and excellent relative valuation. I examined the firm's ratios in detail (see Table 7.6).

I concluded that

- Franklin Resources was the premier asset management firm in the United States as measured by net margin and return on equity.
- The company had very low debt levels and an excellent cover ratio.

(*continued*)

(continued)

TABLE 7.6 Franklin Resources Ratio

2008 E.P.S.	$6.72
Current Ratio	3.3
Debt/Equity	18%
Interest Cover	10.3
Net Margin	36.8%
Price/Sales	2.3
Price/Earnings	8.8
FCF Yield	11.8%
Return on Equity	22.5%

Source: Standard & Poor's.

- The company's trailing P/E ratio was below 9. The historical range was 9–23. The P/S ratio was also very low, at only 2.3. The stock's historical range on a P/S basis was from just over 2 to over 6. With both ratios at trough levels, I felt the downside was limited unless the market collapsed further. Given that the S&P stock index had fallen well over 50% during the past 18 months, I felt the odds of a rebound were elevated.
- The expected growth rate for Franklin Resources was well into the double digits.
- Franklin Resources also had a large percentage of assets in bond mutual funds, thus providing for some stability in revenue and earnings during a very difficult equity fund environment.
- The free cash flow yield was above 11%, offering compelling value on a discounted cash flow basis. The company also maintained over $3 billion in cash on the balance sheet.

(continued)

- The firm sells much of its funds through financial advisors, which in general has allowed for more long-term client relationship. Outflows within the Franklin fund family were below other firms within the industry.

I purchased Franklin Resources for our clients at $48.90 a share in February 2009. The stock rose rapidly during the recovery of 2009, tripling in price by mid-2010. We sold half our position in Franklin to take profits and reduce risk. We added back to our position in October 2011 as the price once again fell below $100 a share. Earnings per share advanced handily, to an expected $8.80 a share by the end of 2011. We continue to keep Franklin Resources in our clients' portfolios as a key financial holding.

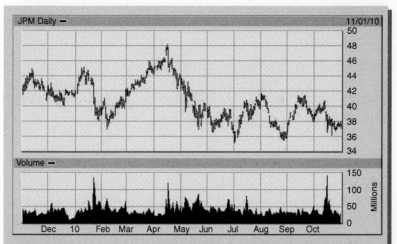

FIGURE 7.2 Case Study No.10: J.P. Morgan Chase, November 2010
Source: Charts provided by Commodity Systems, Inc. (CSI) 2012.

In the summer of 2010, J.P. Morgan Chase's stock was caught in the banking sector downdraft. During the year, the banking sector as measured by the S&P Banking Index

(*continued*)

(*continued*)

TABLE 7.7 J.P. Morgan Chase Ratios

2010 E.P.S.	$3.96
Loans/Assets	31%
Interest Cover	2.04
Book Value	43.4
R.O.E.	9.9%
Price/Earnings	10.0
FCF Yield	9.6%

Source: Standard & Poor's.

had fallen from 165.59 to 118.68. This drop of nearly 30% was due to the continued calamity with the banking industry, including the new regulations being implemented through Dodd–Frank and other various entities. However, I felt that although the new regulations and the lack of loan growth would impact J.P. Morgan Chase stock, the financial sector would rebound during early 2011.

I examined the financial ratios of the company (see Table 7.7).

I arrived at the following conclusions:

- J.P. Morgan Chase was a premier national bank.
- Although the debt levels of the company were still high and liquidity ratios low, it had the best ratios within its own industry.
- The company's president, Jamie Dimon, is considered one of the best CEOs in the banking industry.
- J.P. Morgan Chase's P/E ratio was at 10. The historical range was 9–18. The average P/E over the past 10 years was 13.

(*continued*)

- The expected growth rate for the next five years for JPM was 6%, one of the highest rates within the industry. I felt with loan loss provisions continuing to abate (net charge-offs were expected to be $12.8 billion in 2011, down from 2010's $23.7 billion and 2009's $22.4 billion), by 2012 J.P. Morgan would start to produce accelerating earnings growth.
- It traded at only one times book value, which is considered a floor for most banking stocks. It traded at more than three times book value throughout the past two decades. I felt a reasonable expectation for JPM, with its highly regarded CEO leading the charge, was at least one and a half times book value. That would result in a price target above $50 a share. I set this price target for the end of 2012.

I purchased J.P. Morgan Chase at $36.10 a share for our value portfolios in November 2010 and have continued to hold the shares. The stock suffered along with the financial sector during the first half of 2011, but fared better than the stock of almost every other large U.S. bank.

CHAPTER 8

Bonds, REITs, and Commodities

Good intelligence is nine-tenths of any battle.

Napoleon

In addition to common stocks, other asset classes, such as bonds, real estate, and commodities (including timberland and precious metals) can be an essential part of a diversified investment portfolio. I recommend these investments as a complement to stocks within the five major sectors: health care, consumer staples, energy, technology, and financials. Adding these investments to a portfolio is utilizing a process known as asset allocation. The asset allocation theory (divvying up capital between various stocks, bonds, and cash) dates back to 1952 when Harry Markowitz showed that an asset's risk was related to both its volatility and its correlation with other assets in the portfolio. The Markowitz model was the initial spark for academics to examine the relationship between different assets. Asset allocation gained national prominence after a landmark study conducted in 1986 by Gary P. Brinson, L. Randolph Hood, and Gilbert L. Beebower.[1] These gentlemen found that 93.6% of the total variation in portfolio results was attributable to asset allocation. A follow-up study by Brinson, Beebower, and Brian D. Singer[2] confirmed this result, indicating that asset allocation explained 91.5% of variation in returns. These results underscored the importance of a well-thought-out asset allocation strategy.

Through the 1990s, asset allocation garnered more and more attention. The theory also became more sophisticated. Instead of using just plain vanilla stocks and bonds, financial advisors started including sub-class categories, such as large-cap stocks; small-cap stocks; international and emerging markets stocks; and corporate, government, and foreign bonds. Certain categories, such as commodities, gold, and real estate investments, were also included because they are considered by many to be separate asset classes. In examining other assets for inclusion in a modern portfolio, focus should be placed on the assets' merits. As mentioned in Chapter 2, the addition of international or small-cap stocks does not benefit an investor based on recent evidence of increasing correlations. I feel that only a few asset classes today can add value for an astute investor. These include bonds, liquid real estate (or REITs), and commodities.

Bonds: Corporates Are Worth the Risk

Without bonds as part of a portfolio, investment losses could be a much higher percentage if investment was in stocks alone. Although stocks do generate a higher rate of return over a long period, in the short or immediate term, they may well be outperformed by bonds, especially at critical periods in the economic cycle. Bonds in general are known for the stability and predictability of returns. Bonds, especially those of the government kind, have a low standard deviation (volatility). In fact, bonds are one of the least risky asset classes an investor can own. When combining bonds in a diversified portfolio, you will lower your overall risk. The tradeoff, of course, is the return will be lower than that of an all-stock portfolio.

Most investors have money parked in bonds of the government type (i.e., notes, bills, or bonds). The reason for this has to do with risk and diversification. Government bonds have one of the lowest risk profiles of any asset class and have generally produced consistent returns. Government bonds are also thought to maintain a very low correlation with equities. The long-term average correlation is about 0.09. However, this verity has to be examined on a long-term framework. In fact, correlations between U.S. stocks and Treasuries have swung widely over the past 80 years. The correlation was positive for most of the late 1930s and throughout the 1940s. In the 1950s, the correlation was actually negative as stocks advanced strongly and bonds suffered from declining prices (due to increasing interest rates). From the mid-1960s until 2000 there was a positive correlation, averaging about 0.50.

The correlation turned negative once again during the past decade. This was primarily due to the fact that stocks struggled mightily with two large bear market declines (2002, 2008), while bonds rallied strongly as interest rates declined. So much of the supposed low or negative correlation depends on which time period you examine. The principal problem with owning government bonds is the negative correlation an investor is looking for appears only sporadically throughout history. For this perceived benefit, an investor gives up a substantial amount of return. Is there a better solution than government bonds? I believe there is: corporate bonds.

Corporate bonds are debts issued by a wide variety of U.S. and foreign corporations. Surprisingly, in terms of total face value of bonds outstanding, the corporate bond market is bigger than each of the markets for municipal bonds, U.S. Treasury securities, and government agency securities. Unlike government bonds, corporate bonds are subject to credit risk, which refers to the probability of, and potential loss arising from, a credit event such as defaulting on scheduled payments, filing for bankruptcy, or restructuring. Investors in corporate bonds have an extensive range of selections when it comes to bond maturity, interest rates, credit quality, and provisions. The corporate bond market is generally divided into two markets—bonds that are investment grade and those marked as junk. An investment-grade rating indicates that a corporate bond issuer has a relatively low risk of default. Bond-rating firms, such as Standard & Poor's or Moody's, use different designations consisting of upper- and lower-case letters A and B to identify a bond's credit quality rating. For example, S&P uses AAA and AA as its high credit quality rating, and A and BBB for its medium credit quality rating. These ratings are all considered investment grade. Credit ratings for bonds below these designations (BB, B, CCC, etc.) are considered low credit quality and are commonly referred to as junk bonds. Here are some features of corporate bonds:

- Corporate bonds are hybrids—that is, they maintain a dual nature, both equity and bond. As debt, a bond's value is closely linked to the quality of the issuer, its earnings and revenue, and the likelihood of default. This risk is indicated through the interest rate paid by the issuer.
- Corporate bonds are generally less sensitive to a rise in interest rates.
- Corporate bonds have less liquidity in the capital markets. The lack of liquidity gives rise to market distortions between the value of the bond and its market price. The more uncertain the markets or the economy, the greater the potential distortion in pricing.

Historically, the promised yield on U.S. corporate bonds rated by S&P as AAA (the highest quality bonds issued only by blue-chip companies) has been 0.7% higher (also known as yield spread) than on similar maturity U.S. Treasuries. BBB bonds, the lowest grade bonds deemed by S&P still to be considered investment grade, have a historical yield spread of 1.9% above Treasuries. A key question for investors is not what the typical yield spreads over Treasuries have been, but what returns investors have actually achieved.

To answer this question, I have examined the long-run evidence in detail. Credit Suisse Company publishes a yearbook that examines the long-term returns of various asset classes, including corporate bonds. As the U.S. has consistent corporate bond data going back to 1900, the return subset is quite large. Credit Suisse has found that the long-term return of corporate bonds over 111 years, from 1900 to 2010, was 2.52% per year. This was 0.68% per year more than on U.S. Treasuries. The firm finds these returns very close to the generalized promised yields of AAA bonds, which has averaged 0.70% above Treasury bonds. Published academic research in the past five years also reports the advantage of favoring corporate bonds over Treasuries. Alexander Kozhemiakin (2007)[3] demonstrated in his study published in *The Journal of Portfolio Management* that the excess return of corporate bonds over Treasuries is consistent over time. Furthermore, he found that as investors move to lower-quality bonds, the return differentials become more pronounced. This is especially true in the BB category, where the excess returns are the highest of any grade. The lower tier of the investment-grade spectrum (A/BBB) accounts for two-thirds of the investment-grade market capitalization and trading activity. The excess returns over U.S. Treasuries are listed in Table 8.1, and long-term returns versus other primary bond indices are presented in Table 8.2.

TABLE 8.1 Annualized Excess Return over U.S. Treasuries

Rating	Return	Excess Return over U.S. Treasuries
AAA/AA Rating	8.9%	1.4%
A Rating	9.2%	1.7%
BBB Rating	9.3%	1.8%
BB Rating	11.0%	3.3%
B Rating	9.7%	2.0%
CCC Rating	2.8%	−2.7%

Source: Kozhemiakin, A. (2007). "The Risk Premium of Corporate Bonds." *The Journal of Portfolio Management*, Barclay's, 101–109.

TABLE 8.2 Performance of BB High-Yield Bonds vs. Index

	5 Year	10 Years	20 Years
BB Rated Bonds	9.29%	8.78%	9.63%
Barclay's Aggregate Bond Index	6.52%	5.74%	6.80%
Barclay's Govt. Bond Index	5.62%	4.87%	5.76%

Source: Credit Suisse.

Corporate Bonds Risk Components

An investor should expect corporate bonds to trade at higher yields than Treasury bonds over extended periods of time. The primary difference between the two yields is known as the credit spread. However, credit risk is not the only factor in determining the excess returns of corporate bonds over government bonds. Other key factors include tax treatment, illiquidity, and the unique provisions that are included in the contracts of corporate bonds. These are characteristics that government bonds do not share. Although most investors will look at the excess returns as coming from pure credit risk, academic research has concluded otherwise. Credit risk is in fact not the primary factor in explaining excess returns. Jing-zhi Huang of Penn State University and Ming Huang of Stanford found that within the investment grade bond arena, less than one-third of the excess return was associated with default risk.[4] Additional studies confirm these findings. Professors Gordon Delianedis and Robert Geske of The Anderson School at UCLA found that for AAA-rated firms, only a small fraction (5%) could be attributed to actual default risk. For BBB-rated firms, which are those rated just above junk, only 22% of the credit spread can be attributed to default risk. The team further concluded that credit risk and credit spreads above government bonds are not primarily explained by default, leverage, or a firm's specific risk but are primarily attributable to taxes, jumps, liquidity, and market-risk factors.[5]

It is interesting to view whether these studies are consistent with actual default rates. According to the aforementioned Credit Suisse yearbook, default rates for all rated corporate bond issuers since 1900 have averaged 1.14% per year, while for riskier high-yield bonds, the average was 2.8%. Of course over certain chaotic economic periods the default rate has reached much higher extremes. Default rates were at the highest levels following the Great Depression at 8.4% in 1933 for high-grade bonds, while high-yield bonds had a default rate that year of 15.4%. The default rate for all corporate bonds reached 3.7% in the recession of 2001. The second-worst episode for default rates followed the recent credit crisis, and in 2009, the default rate on all rated bonds was 5.4%, while that on high-yield bonds was just over 13%. Given the low default rates over history, a long-run return premium of 0.68% per year for the highest grade, AAA, seems puzzlingly high. For the riskier element of the corporate bond market, a 3% plus premium for BB bonds seems downright generous, given the fact that the annual default rate for these bonds is less than 3%. Furthermore, many researchers have found the 3% default rate for bonds on the edge of junk status, BB, is overstated. Stephen Kealhofer, Sherry Kwok, and Wenlong Weng found that true default rates for AAA bonds were only 0.13%, while even the riskier BB rating category showed a default rate of only 1.42%.[6]

Part of this credit premium is undoubtedly a risk of default premium, but given that the actual risk of nonpayment has been quite low, it seems likely that other factors are at work. One primary theory for why the wide yield spread for corporate bonds persists is the typical illiquidity of these bonds. The foundation for excess returns is that the illiquidity of corporate bonds has a larger-than-customary effect. Although corporate bonds are traded widely on markets such as the New York Stock

Exchange, the volume of transactions is far less than for government bonds. Since increased liquidity is an attractive quality of any investment, investors will thus demand extra remuneration for holding securities that are less liquid and thus more expensive to sell. For corporate bonds, this illiquidity premium shows up in higher interest-rate spreads over otherwise comparable government securities. That is the theory of several prominent researchers. Patrick Houweling, Albert Mentink, and Ton Vorst (2005) analyzed the effect of liquidity risk on corporate bond credit spreads based on a sample of 999 investment-grade corporate bonds.[7] In their paper, they controlled two common factors: (1) the excess return from the stock market and (2) the excess return of long-term corporate bonds over long-term Treasury bonds in addition to the rating and maturity of each bond. They found that liquidity risk is priced into credit spreads and does explain a significant portion of observed credit risk spreads.

In addition to liquidity risk, corporate bonds have a substantial amount of volatility risk. This is because although actual default risk is below expectations, default is most likely to take place in recessions. While relatively protected for most economic periods, corporate bonds thus become a far riskier asset in severe recessions. This was demonstrated emphatically in the deep recession of 2008–2009. Corporate bonds returned a negative 21% in 2008, while the Barclay's U.S. 5–10-Year Treasury Index returned 16.77%. Many advisors argue the corporate bond asset class is less appropriate for long-term investors who hold a substantial portion of equity in their portfolio because other fixed-income asset classes (namely government bonds) do a better job reducing the risk of the overall portfolio. In 2008, holding Treasury bonds over corporate bonds would have resulted in a substantial reduction in portfolio volatility. However, in 2009, corporate bonds excelled and rebounded strongly alongside stocks. If an investor can withstand the extra volatility, especially during recessions, then corporate bonds will ultimately be the best asset class to own. It is especially rewarding if investors concentrate their corporate bond holdings within the BBB and BB ratings universe. These bonds typically will reward a bond investor with a 3% annualized premium over a government bond of the same duration.

Trading individual corporate bonds is not like trading stocks. Stocks can be bought at uniform prices and are traded through exchanges. Most bonds trade over the counter, and individual brokers price them. Price transparency has improved over the past decade. In 1999, the bond markets gained transparency from the House of Representatives' Bond Price Competition Improvement Act of 1999. Responding to this pioneering law, the site www.investinginbonds.com was established. This site provides current prices on bonds that have traded more than four times the previous day. With the advent of investinginbonds.com and real-time reporting of many trades, investors are much better off today. Many well-regarded brokers, including Schwab, Ameritrade, and Fidelity Investments, now have dedicated websites devoted to bond trading and pricing. Fidelity Investments chose to disclose its fee structure for all corporate bonds, making it clear what it will cost per trade. Fidelity charges $1 per bond trade. Some online brokers charge a flat fee as well, ranging from $10.95 at Zions Direct to $45 at TD Ameritrade. Depending on the number of bonds trading, one may be more complementary than another. The trading fee disclosures, however, do not divulge the spreads between the buy and sell price embedded in the transaction that some dealer is making in the channel. Keep in mind that only comparison shopping can assist you in finding the best transaction price, after all fees have been taken into account. Other sites may not charge any fee but will embed the profit in the spread.

Despite the difficulty in pricing and transparency, investing in individual corporate bonds offers several rewards over purchasing bond mutual funds. First, you know exactly what you will be receiving in interest each year. You will also know the exact maturity date. Furthermore, your individual investment is protected against interest-rate risk, at least over the full term to maturity. Both individual bonds and bond funds share interest-rate risk—that is, the risk of locking up an investment at a given rate only to see rates rise. This pushes bond prices down. At least with an individual bond, you can reinvest it at the higher, market rate once the bond matures. But the lack of a fixed maturity date on a bond mutual fund causes an open-ended problem—there is no promise of getting the original investment back.

Short of default, an individual bond will return all principal and pay all interest, assuming you hold it to maturity. Bond funds are not likely to default as most funds maintain positions in hundreds of individual bonds. The force of interest-rate risk to both individual bond or bond mutual fund prices depends on the maturity of a bond investment: the longer the maturity of a bond or bond fund (average), the more the price will drop due to rising rates. Duration, a statistical term that measures the price sensitivity to yield, is the primary measurement of a bond or bond fund's sensitivity to interest-rate changes. Duration indicates approximately how much the price of a bond or bond fund will adjust in the reverse direction given a rise in interest rates. For instance, an individual bond with an average duration of five years will fall in value approximately 5% if rates rise by 1%, and the opposite is true as well.

By purchasing individual bonds, an investor will not incur the continuing management and operating expenses of bond funds. The issue of ownership costs of individual bonds versus bond funds was examined by the Schwab Center for Investment Research in 1999. Schwab found that the cost for investors who hold individual Treasury, corporate, or municipal bonds at least five years is on par or even lower than comparable costs for buying low-cost bond funds—if the investor owns at least $50,000 in worth of individual bonds. The problem for many investors is that the amount of funds available to purchase individual bonds may prevent them from sufficiently diversifying among dissimilar issues. Holding a minimum of $50,000 in individual bonds thus is a proper approach. At this level of assets, an individual could purchase bonds of at least 20 different issuers. Table 8.3 shows a sample portfolio holding individual bonds in the BBB and BB ratings category;

TABLE 8.3 Corporate Bond Sample Portfolio

Issuer	Price
ALBERTSONS 7.45% 08/1/2029	$98.73
ANADARKO PETROLEUM 6.45% 09/15/2036	$115.51
CIGNA CORP NT 7.65% 03/01/2023	$117.34
GOLDMAN SACHS 5.95% 01/15/2027	$98.57
HCA INC NT 6.25% 02/15/2013	$104.00
HERTZ CORP NT 7.625% 06/01/2012	$103.75
HOME DEPOT INC 5.40% 03/01/2016	$112.84
HONEYWELL INTL 6.125% 11/01/2011	$101.54
HUMANA INC BONDS 6.30% 08/01/2018	$111.84
INTUIT INC BONDS 5.75% 03/15/2017	$113.27
LIMITED 7.00% 5/1/2020	$107.50
MGM RESORTS 5.875% 02/27/2014	$97.37
MARRIOTT INTL INC 5.81% 11/10/2015	$111.18
MASCO CORP NOTES 07.125% 03/15/2020	$101.92
MERRILL LYNCH CO 5.00% 01/15/2015	$105.09
PENNEY J C CORP 5.75% 02/15/2018	$102.00
PRUDENTIAL FINL 5.10% 09/20/2014	$110.03
SOUTHWEST AIR 5.125% 03/01/2017	$108.15
SPRINT CAP 6.875% 11/15/2019	$96.75
SUNTRUST BKS 6.00% 02/15/2026	$100.35
VALERO ENRGY 6.125% 02/01/2020	$112.71
VERIZON COMM 5.55% 02/15/2016	$114.39
WELLPOINT INC 5.25% 01/15/2016	$112.64
WENDYS INTL 6.200% 06/15/2014	$105.00

Source: Standard & Poor's.

The sample corporate bond portfolio above is laddered. A bond ladder is a portfolio of bonds with alternate maturities. Your goal in building such a ladder is to reduce the reinvestment risk of rolling over all your maturing bonds at once. By staggering the date of maturity, you will be able to continually keep up with interest rates. This is especially critical if interest rates rise. As interest rates would rise, you would have the capability to rollover to a new bond with a higher guaranteed rate of return. Additionally, by spreading out your purchases of individual corporate bonds, you may choose coupon dates and have control over when interest payments are made.

More than 90% of the total return since 1976 generated from a broadly balanced portfolio of U.S. investment-grade Treasury, agency, and corporate bonds has come from interest payments as opposed to change in price.[8] However, price can make a difference as bond prices move inversely to interest rates. If interest rates rise, bond prices will fall. For example, the corporate bonds listed in Table 8.3 were all issued at par value, or $1,000. If the $1,000 bond is issued with an initial coupon (interest) rate of 5%, payments would be $50 per year to the security holder. If interest rates increase to 8% in the bond markets, then the supposed value of the purchased bond will decrease. The reason is an investor would never pay $1,000 for a bond that pays $50 a year in interest when that investor could purchase a new security offering $70 a year in interest (coupon of 8%). In order to stay competitive with a new bond issued at 7% interest, the former bond holder must discount his or her bond. And the discount can be substantial. To equal out and provide a buyer of the 5% coupon bond with the proper discount, the price of the bond would have to decrease to ($50/0.08) or $625.00. Most bond investors fail to realize that their bonds, much like stocks, can decline in value. One caveat—if an investor holds the bond to maturity, he or she will always be guaranteed (as long as the issuer does not default) the original $1,000 face value. This is the one strong advantage of holding individual bonds over bond mutual funds. Mutual funds can never promise the original investment back, as there is no guarantee at maturity.

I strongly advise that if you do have a larger portfolio, purchasing individual corporate bonds is the best method to protect your portfolio against the ravages of higher interest rates and principal loss.

REITs: A Separate Asset Class?

In case you have not yet heard, real estate investment trusts (REITs) were promoted from being just a small industry group to a full-fledged asset class. They even skipped right over being a sector, as I don't recall the Global Industry Classification Standard (GICS) adding an eleventh category. This must be the case, because everywhere I look, mutual fund wrap programs and asset allocation shops are including a separate and distinct allocation just for REITs. REITs are merely an industry that is part of the financial sector, alongside banks and insurance companies, to name two. They are primarily value oriented and tend to be small- and mid-cap names. They make up approximately 10% of the overall financial sector, which is roughly 20% to 25% of the overall domestic equity market. Just shy of 200 REITs are registered with the SEC and trade on one of the major stock exchanges (the majority on the NYSE). As of the end of the fourth quarter of this year there were 11 REITs in the S&P 500 Index. What is a REIT? A REIT, or real estate investment trust, is a company that buys, develops, manages, and sells real estate assets. REITs are actually considered equity products, or stock. However, in this text I list them under the "other" component category. This is due to their high dividends or yield, and their unique relationship with equities. REITs basically allow participants to invest in a professionally managed portfolio of real estate properties. Typically, REITs concentrate on one type: apartments, offices, shopping malls, hotels, and even storage units.

The attraction for investors is two-fold. First, REITs offer a chance to own a diversified piece of choice properties that could appreciate in value—especially if inflation returns. Second, these companies are required by law to pay out 90% of the rents they collect in the form of dividends to shareholders. Therefore, many REITs have dividend yields of 4% or more, which is very attractive in today's low-interest investment environment. REITs qualify as pass-through entities, companies that are able to distribute the majority of income cash flows to investors without taxation at the corporate level. As pass-through entities, whose main function is to pass profits on to investors, a REIT's business activities are generally restricted to generation of property rental income.

As mentioned, the primary benefit of a REIT investment instead of traditional private ownership is its liquidity (ease of liquidation of assets into cash). One reason for the liquid nature of REIT investments is that its shares are traded primarily on major stock exchanges, making it very easy to buy and sell REIT assets/ shares. More than 180 REITs are publicly traded, with market capitalization topping $170 billion. In considering REITs as an alternative investment choice, an investor should examine two important criteria. One, they must provide above-average investment returns over time. Two, they must provide diversification benefits to an overall portfolio. Fortunately, REITs provide both qualities.

The compound overall return of REITs is attractive. According to data provided by the NAREIT association, REIT stocks have registered a compound annual total return of 11.87 percent from 1980 through 2010. The combination of income returns from dividends and capital gains from share price appreciation can result in healthy overall returns for REIT investors. The average REIT that trades on the New York Stock Exchange paid out a 4% yield in the form of a cash dividend in 2011. One advantage of owning REIT shares is the expected low correlation with other major asset classes, especially large-company stocks and bonds. REIT correlations were in the 60% range throughout the 1970s and 1980s. In the mid 1990s, REIT correlations diverged from U.S. stocks, and by 2004 the average 10-year correlation statistic had dropped to 27%. Investment advisors then jumped on the REIT bandwagon, as not only was the correlation dropping, but the average returns over the previous decade were extremely strong. But over the past few years, REIT correlations with U.S. stocks have risen to nearly 65%. Over the 20-year period from 1990 to 2010, the annual return correlation between REITs and the U.S. stock market was 0.49.

Many pundits argue that investing in REITs is quite similar to investing in small-company stocks. However, the data dispels this myth. Over the past decade, the correlation to small-company stocks is actually lower than to large-company stocks. There are several reasons for the lower level of correlation. Many real estate lease agreements are entered into for years at a time, so rentals continue without regard to short-term economic swings. As a result, real estate values appear to lag the economic market cycle. Small-company stocks tend to lead the economy, not lag it. In addition, because sales are infrequent, many institutional investors rely on appraisals to value a REIT. These appraisals appear to smooth the market value of the properties, understating volatility.

In addition to low correlation, REITs also provide some degree of inflation protection. NAREIT has demonstrated that REITs have historically provided reliable inflation hedging, with total returns meeting or exceeding the inflation rate 65.8 percent of the time, versus only 60.4% for the S&P 500 Index. In short, a lower-risk (more diversified) portfolio that included REITs trumped the general market.

Commodities and Gold

Although it may sound frightening and risky to many investors, if handled correctly, commodities including gold can be an integral piece of an investor's portfolio. What exactly are commodities? Commodities are any mass goods traded on an exchange or in a cash market including cocoa, coffee, eggs, lumber, orange juice, soybeans, and sugar, just to name a few. Industrial metals are also included, with gold, copper, aluminum, zinc, nickel, silver, and lead ranking among the most popular industrial metals holdings. They are traded in order to profit from the fluctuation in price from these basic goods. These potential profits result from the buying or selling of futures contracts in a particular good. A commodities futures contract is an obligation to purchase a commodity at a given price and time. For instance, an investor could purchase a contract that obligates him to buy sugar in June at a stated price. Money is made when the price of sugar rises, thus increasing the demand of that contract because it allows the investor to purchase sugar at a lower price. Commodities are traded on an exchange or in a cash market. The Chicago Board of Trade (CBOT), the Chicago Mercantile Exchange (CME), and the London Mercantile Exchange (LME) are among the most popular futures exchanges. Commodities provide a play on globalization by their ability to aid in the improvement of the global economy. This is because prices for industrial materials will increase as demand for industrial goods increase. As countries such as China and other emerging market economies develop, they will require more raw staples. This is especially true for industrial metals. China continues to develop at a rapid pace and consequently, its demand for raw materials continues to rise. In fact, China's iron ore demand has increased from 5% of the world's supply to almost 50% over the past 12 years.

Gold is a monetary metal whose price is determined by inflation, by fluctuations in the dollar and U.S. stocks, by currency-related crises, interest-rate volatility and international tensions, and by increases or decreases in the prices of other commodities. The price of gold reacts to supply and demand changes and can be influenced by consumer spending and overall levels of affluence. Gold is different from other precious metals such as platinum, palladium, and silver, because the demand for these precious metals arises principally from their industrial applications. Gold is produced primarily for accumulation; other commodities are produced primarily for consumption. Gold's value does not arise from its usefulness in industrial or consumable applications. It arises from its use and worldwide acceptance as a store of value. Gold is money. In contrast to other commodities, gold does not perish, tarnish or corrode, nor does gold have quality grades. Over very long time periods each investment class cycles between massive undervaluation and massive overvaluation. During the late 1970s, for example, burgeoning fears of inflation and plummeting confidence in the monetary system caused a spectacular surge in the investment demand for gold and caused stock market participants to assign very low multiples to company earnings and dividends.

As stocks took off in the 1980s, gold collapsed and basically went through a 20-year bear market. In fact, gold has not been a good long-term investment. The previous peak was about $850 an ounce in 1980. Anyone who had squirreled some gold coins away in a safety deposit box back then would have made next to nothing over 28 years. Indeed, with inflation factored in, gold has lost value over that period. Wharton finance professor Jeremy Siegel reported that a dollar invested in gold in 1801 would have grown to just $1.95 at the end of 2006, while a dollar put into a basket of stocks reflecting the entire stock market would have grown to more than $755,000. Despite the poor long-term record of gold, I do believe that it provides a hedge against the stock market, especially when inflation is rampant.

It also is a component of the commodities index, which I also believe adds value to a diversified portfolio.

In building a commodity weight for your portfolio, you can use a different methodology than the GSCI commodity index to produce the same results. When you examine the index, it maintains a weight of 70% in energy. Add in precious metals, which accounts for 15% of the index, and you account for nearly the entire GSCI weighting. A recent study performed by Craig Israelsen at Brigham Young University examined this strategy. Examining the 20-year period from 1987 through 2007, he found that a mixture of Vanguard Energy, Fidelity Real Estate, and Vanguard Metals and Mining improved the return of a typical stock and bond portfolio while reducing risk. It also provided an improved return and reduced risk compared to a conventional portfolio with a GSCI Commodities Index component. The correlation of this mix of funds was very close to the actual commodities index. The other advantage with a "do-it-yourself" approach is costs. Commodity funds are notoriously expensive due to their complex nature. These funds generally use derivatives, futures contracts, and structured notes. All of these methods escalate the costs for the funds, which then have to pass on the expense to shareholders.

Overall, the thought process behind adding commodities to a portfolio of assets is rational. Commodities offer solid long-term returns and have a low correlation with other assets. But you can get the same type of diversification by utilizing other investments that are more cost-effective. I recommend a combination of our recommended energy stocks with gold and a small amount of REITs.

CHAPTER 9

Fundamental Analysis

Great intellects are skeptical.

Nietzsche

Fundamental analysis involves the use of financial and economic data to evaluate a company. Notice that the title of this chapter is not "Stock Analysis." Though evaluating a stock is the most common phrase used when performing research, your focus should be on evaluating a business. Before ever buying stock, you must access the fundamental condition of the business itself. If the business passes several key tests, you can examine the stock to determine whether it is reasonably valued.

The future of each share of company stock is always tied inextricably to the fortune of the underlying business and the market's perception of the future prospects for that business. As an astute analyst, you must basically answer three key questions:

- Is this a financially sound company?
- Is this company a financial leader in its industry?
- Is the company's stock priced attractively right now?

If the answer to all three questions is yes, you have identified an engaging stock candidate. You start the process by evaluating the liquidity, solvency, efficiency and, most importantly, the earnings potential of a given company. To determine this, you will depend on a financial analyst's toolkit, which includes the corporation's annual report, 10K and 10Q, independent analysts' research reports, and macro-economic data. With this information in hand, your goal is to thoroughly examine a company and ultimately answer the three questions. This is not an easy process. While it is not critical for the average investor to fully understand every aspect of financial statement analysis, it is necessary to have a broad understanding of what appears within a company's financial statements. Investors who can perform good fundamental analysis and spot pricing discrepancies will be able to build a portfolio of superlative stocks.

Before we begin evaluating the different approaches to common stock evaluation, a quick review of a firm's primary financial statements is needed. There are two major financial statements that an investor must review before undertaking the task of stock evaluation.

The Balance Sheet and the Income Statement

This section is designed to teach you some basic methods for analyzing both the balance sheet and the income statement. Analyzing both statements is an important tool to help investors appraise their investment options.

Balance Sheet Analysis

The analysis of a balance sheet is done to identify potential liquidity problems. These may signify the company's inability to meet financial obligations. An investor also can examine the degree to which a company is leveraged, or indebted. An overly leveraged company may have difficulties raising future capital. Even more severe, they may be headed towards bankruptcy.

These are just a few of the danger signs that can be detected with careful analysis of a balance sheet.

As an investor, you will want to know whether a company you are considering is in danger of not being able to make its payments. After all, some of the company's obligations will be to you if you choose to invest in it. To find out, you should turn to several of the most fundamental financial ratios. The first is the current ratio. The current ratio measures a firm's ability to pay its current obligations. The greater the extent to which current assets exceed current liabilities, the more easily a company can meet its short-term obligations.

$$\text{current ratio} = \text{current assets}/\text{current liabilities}$$

After calculating the current ratio for a company, you should compare it with other companies in the same industry. A ratio lower than that of the industry average suggests that the company may have liquidity problems. Most accountants claim that a ratio of 2.0 (twice as many current assets as current liabilities) is a good benchmark, but it depends on the business. High-growth companies need a larger cushion to finance rapid expansion, while big, established firms can get away with less. Attention should also be paid to the current ratio trend over time. A low, but stable current ratio is less of a problem than a sharply declining ratio that might signal either unsustainable growth or a deteriorating business. Both conditions are serious red flags for any investor.

The quick ratio (also known as the acid test) is very similar to the current ratio except that it excludes inventory. For this reason, it is also a more conservative ratio.

$$\text{quick ratio} = \text{current assets} - \text{inventory}/\text{current liabilities}$$

Inventory is excluded in this ratio because, in many industries, inventory cannot be quickly converted to cash. Sometimes, the value of the inventory is inflated or perhaps even worthless.

If this is the case, inventory should not be included as an asset that can be used to pay off short-term obligations. As with the current ratio, to have a quick ratio at or above the industry average is desirable. A quick ratio over 1 shows proper liquidity. Working capital is an additional measure of liquidity. It is the amount by which current assets exceed current liabilities. Here it is in the form of an equation:

$$\text{working capital} = \text{current assets} - \text{current liabilities}$$

This formula is very similar to the current ratio. The only difference is it gives you a dollar amount rather than a ratio. It is calculated to determine a firm's ability to pay its short-term obligations. Positive working capital can be viewed as somewhat of a security blanket. The greater the amount of working capital, the more security an investor can have that the firm will be able to meet financial obligations.

Another critical element of a firm's financial condition is its debt characteristics. The long-term debt-to-equity ratio measures a company's capital structure. In other words, it measures how a company finances its assets on a long-term basis.

$$\text{long-term debt-to-equity ratio} = \text{long-term debt}/\text{total equity}$$

A firm that finances its assets with a high percentage of debt is potentially risking bankruptcy. This may happen if the economy struggles or the business does not perform as well as expected. A firm with a lower percentage of debt has a bigger safety cushion should times turn bad. A related side effect of being highly leveraged is the unwillingness of lenders to provide more debt financing. In this case, a firm that finds itself in a jam may have to issue stock on unfavorable terms. All in all, being highly leveraged is generally viewed as disadvantageous due to the increased risk of bankruptcy, higher borrowing costs, and decreased financial flexibility. On the other hand, using debt financing does have advantages. Stockholders' potential return on their investment is greater when a firm borrows more. Borrowing also has some tax advantages. Overall, a company that is highly leveraged adds another layer of risk for a stockholder.

Income Statement Analysis

The income statement is important for investors because it is the basic measuring stick of profitability. A company with little or no income has little chance of future growth or money to pass on to its investors in the form of dividends. If a company continues to record losses for a sustained period, it could easily go bankrupt. By analyzing an income statement properly, you can begin to evaluate the effectiveness of the management on the operations of the firm. Proper income sheet analysis can help identify worthy investment opportunities. It can also reduce the risk involved with choosing a poor investment. Assuming the firm checks out for reasonable financial soundness in the balance sheet analysis, you may then turn your attention to the bottom line of the income statement—earnings per share (E.P.S.). This figure represents the total net income divided by the number of shares the firm has issued.

E.P.S. = net income/number of shares outstanding

Think of E.P.S. as your share of the corporation's overall profit if it paid everything out to the stockholders and kept nothing to reinvest in the business. If the earnings are declining over time or jump around unpredictably, the company in question can have serious problems. Many industries, such as autos or airlines, are subject to the business cycle and have dramatic swings in earnings per share. The more stable a firm's E.P.S. is over time, the less overall risk you assume as an investor.

Few things will panic investors more than a company that is unable to make its interest payments. That is why it is critical to ensure that the firm can meet the demands of its creditors even during a temporary downturn. A method to calculate these demands is the interest coverage ratio. It takes the earnings before interest and taxes (EBIT) and divides it by the interest expense to figure out how many times over the interest payments could be met with current income. It gives you a sense of how far a company's earnings can fall before it will start defaulting on its bond payments.

$$\text{interest coverage} = \text{earnings before interest and taxes}/\text{interest payments}$$

Look for companies that are able to cover their interest charges at least three to four times over. As a general rule of thumb, investors should not own a stock that has an interest coverage ratio under 2. An interest coverage ratio below 1.0 indicates the business is having difficulties generating the cash necessary to pay its interest obligations. The history and consistency of earnings is tremendously important. The more consistent a company's earnings, the lower the acceptable interest coverage ratio can be. The higher this ratio, the more safety built into the stock.

Next you should examine profit margins. There are several different ratios to research: gross profit margin, operating profit margin, and net profit margin. Profitability is often measured in percentage terms in order to facilitate making comparisons of a company's financial performance against past year's performance and against the performance of other companies. When profitability is expressed as a percentage (or ratio), the new figures are called profit margins. The most common profit margins are all expressed as percentages of net sales. Let's look at a few of the most commonly used profit margins you can easily learn to use to help you measure and compare firms:

$$\text{gross profit margin} = \text{gross profit}/\text{total sales}$$

Since this ratio takes into account only sales and variable costs (costs of goods sold), it's a good indicator of a firm's efficiency in producing and distributing its products. A firm with a ratio superior to the industry average demonstrates superior efficiency in its production processes. The higher the ratio, the higher the efficiency of the production process. Within certain industries, the gross margin is not relevant. This is because many companies do not have a cost-of-goods-sold line. As the name implies, operating margin is the resulting ratio when operating income is divided by net sales.

$$\text{operating profit margin} = \text{operating profit/total sales}$$

This ratio measures the quality of a firm's operations. A firm with a high operating margin in relation to the industry average has operations that are more efficient. Typically, to achieve this result, the company must have lower fixed costs, a better gross margin, or a combination of the two. At any rate, companies that are more efficient than their competitors in their core operations have a distinct advantage. The last profitability measure we will cover in this section is net margin. As the name implies, net margin is a measure of profitability for the sum of a firm's operations.

$$\text{net profit margin} = \text{net profit/total sales}$$

As with the other ratios you will want to compare net margin with that of other companies in the industry. You can also track year-to-year changes in net margin to see if a company's competitive position is improving or getting worse. The higher the net margin relative to the industry (or relative to past years), the better. Often a high net margin indicates that the company you are looking at is an efficient producer with a dominant position in its industry. However, as with all the previous profit margin measurements, you need to always check past years of performance. You want to make sure that good results are not a fluke. Strong profit margins that are sustainable indicate that a company has been able to consistently outperform its competitors. The savvy investor uses profitability margins to help analyze income statements of prospective investments. Companies with high interest coverage ratios, gross margins, operating margins, and net margins will always be very attractive to investors.

Once you have completed the balance sheet and income statement analysis, your attention should be focused on six key financial valuation statistics, which are discussed in the following subsections.

1. PRICE/EARNINGS RATIO   P/E ratio was discussed in Chapter 1. To review, it is one of the oldest and most frequently used metrics when it comes to valuing stocks. This is the earnings per share divided by the average primary shares outstanding over the past 12 months.

price/earnings ratio = price of share of stock/E.P.S.

The P/E ratio gives you an indication of a stock's value. If it is low (though some sectors tend to be chronically low), it usually means that the stock price reflects a reasonable valuation relative to the earnings stream. If it is high (though some sectors tend to be chronically high), it usually means that the stock price reflects a high valuation relative to the earnings stream. Most of the time, the P/E is calculated using E.P.S. from the most recent four quarters. This is also known as the trailing P/E. However, it can also be used by estimating the E.P.S. figure expected over the next four quarters. This is known as the leading or forward P/E. A third variation is sometimes used that consists of the past two quarters and estimates of the next two quarters. There is not a huge difference between these variations. It is important you realize that you are using actual historical data for the calculation in the first case. The other two are based on analyst estimates that are not always perfect or precise.

The P/E ratio is a much better indicator of the value of a stock than the market price alone. For example, all things being equal, a $10 stock with a P/E of 75 is much more expensive than a $100 stock with a P/E of 20. Therefore, the P/E ratio allows you to compare two different companies with two different market prices—comparing "apples to apples," so to speak. A potential problem with the P/E involves companies that are not profitable and consequently have a negative E.P.S. There are varying opinions on how to deal with this. I recommend that if a firm does not have a P/E due to depressed earnings, an investor should use an alternative valuation model, such as the price/sales ratio. It is difficult to state whether a particular P/E is high or low without taking into account two main factors:

Company Growth Rates   A P/E is primarily based on the growth rate of the prospective company. Generally, the higher the growth rate, the higher the expected P/E. If the projected growth rate does not justify the P/E, a stock might be overpriced.

Industry   Comparing P/E ratios of companies is much more beneficial if they are in the same industry. For example, auto companies typically have low P/E ratios because they possess low earnings growth. In contrast, the technology industry is characterized by high growth rates. Comparing an auto firm to a technology stalwart is fruitless. You should concentrate on comparing companies with their competitors. This is known as relative valuation.

Historically, the average P/E ratio in the market has been around 15. This fluctuates significantly depending on economic conditions at the time. Periods of high inflation are generally marked with low P/E ratios. Alternatively, periods of low inflation are signified by high P/E ratios.

2. PRICE/SALES RATIO   This ratio is the total revenue (sales) divided by the average primary shares outstanding over the past 12 months. It also gives an indication of value. If it is low, it usually means that the stock price reflects a reasonable valuation relative to the revenue stream. If it is high, it usually means that the stock price reflects a high valuation relative to the revenue stream. I recommend the P/S ratio as an alternative valuation tool, especially when a firm has no P/E ratio.

price/sales = price of share of stock/sales per share

3. PEG RATIO The relationship between the price/earnings ratio and earnings growth tells a much more complete story than the P/E on its own. This is called the Price/Earnings/ Growth Ratio (PEG). PEG is formulated as follows:

PEG ratio = P/E ratio/annual expected 5-yr E.P.S. growth

The PEG ratio compares a stock's price/earnings (P/E) ratio to its expected E.P.S growth rate. I use the expected growth rate over the next five years as the denominator. Of course, predicting the five-year growth rate is quite difficult. It is an inexact science. Generally, an assumed five-year growth rate is based on both the past growth and the future potential of the firm. If the PEG ratio is equal to one, it means that the market is pricing the stock to fully reflect the stock's E.P.S growth. If the PEG ratio is greater than one, it indicates that the stock is evaluated above its growth rate or possibly that the market anticipates future E.P.S growth to be superior. If the PEG ratio is less than one, it is a sign of a possibly undervalued stock or that the market does not expect the company to achieve the earnings growth that is reflected in the Wall Street estimates. It is important to note that the PEG ratio cannot be used in isolation. As with all financial ratios, to properly use PEG ratios, investors must compare PEG ratios among companies in the same industry. The firms with the highest PEG ratios are ordinarily the market leaders. Ranking industries by their PEG or P/E ratios creates a so-called totem pole where each company falls into place based on its future outlook.

Amazingly, the PEG ratio for the S&P 500 Index currently stands at 1.75. Therefore, investors are willing to pay $1.75 for every \$1.00 in potential earnings. You should look for investment candidates that possess low PEG ratios.

4. RETURN ON ASSETS

$$R.O.A. = \text{net income/average total assets}$$

R.O.A. is calculated by the profit generated per sales dollar times the sales generated per dollar of assets. This is a measure of how well the company deploys the assets it has. It may have a small asset base from which it generates big revenues. This would be a successful operation. If, however, the company needs added assets to show profit, it may need to reassess the business. Return on assets measures a company's earnings in relation to all of the resources it has at its disposal (the shareholders' capital plus short- and long-term borrowed funds). Thus, it is the most stringent test of return to shareholders.

The lower the profit per dollar of assets, the more asset-intensive a business is. The higher the profit per dollar of assets, the less asset-intensive a business is. All things being equal, the more asset-intensive a business, the more money must be reinvested into it to continue generating earnings. If a company has an R.O.A. of 20%, it means that the company earned \$0.20 for each \$1 in assets. As a general rule, anything below 5% is very asset-heavy (e.g., manufacturing, railroads). Anything above 20% is asset-light (e.g., advertising firms, software companies). As with all other financial ratios, it is critical to examine the R.O.A. of companies within the same industry.

5. RETURN ON EQUITY

$$R.O.E. = \text{net income/shareholder equity}$$

Return on equity is the available common stock income after all expenses, excluding common stock dividends, then divided by the average common stock equity (also called the net worth).

This is expressed as a percentage and is a measure of how effectively a company's earnings stream is being deployed. R.O.E. is one of the most important profitability metrics. Return on equity reveals how much profit a company earned in comparison to the total amount of shareholder equity found on the balance sheet. A business that has a high return on equity is more likely to be capable of generating significant cash internally. For the most part, the higher a company's return on equity compared with others in its industry, the better. For most of the 20th century, the S&P 500 Index averaged R.O.E.s of 10 to 15%. During the 1990s, the average return on equity was in excess of 20%. Of course, this was an anomaly. Expect the average R.O.E. to return to the long-term averages. All other things being equal, a higher number denotes better use of funds.

6. FREE CASH FLOW YIELD RATIO

F.C.F.Y. = free cash flow per share/price of share

This ratio examines a firm's ability to generate cash earnings. It is computed in two steps. The first is taking the trailing 12-month free cash flow divided by the trailing 12-month average number of shares outstanding; the second is taking this result and dividing it by the current stock price. The reason you should differentiate free cash flow from regular earnings is that companies have non-earnings items such as depletion allowances, depreciation credits, interest accrued but not yet paid, tax overpayments, and so on. Free cash flow speaks to the actual dollars a company generates after capital expenditures. It measures the company's true ability to pay its bills and its dividends. This ratio is one of my favorites. It examines what investment return you would earn if you owned every share of outstanding stock and all cash earnings were paid out to you. If a company generates a 1% F.C.F. yield, would you buy out the company? Hopefully, your answer is no. Therefore, you should also avoid the stock.

By applying minimum standards on a F.C.F. yield, you will avoid buying businesses that are extremely overvalued. All of the Internet stocks of the late 1990s had either scant or negative F.C.F. yields. Why did their stocks continue to go up? Investors simply did not value these companies properly; they were caught up in the hype. Once the hype ran out, these stocks came back to earth, or in many cases ventured into bankruptcy. Any stock you consider should have a F.C.F. yield higher than that of a bond. This recommendation is just common sense. Since you incur added risk by purchasing a stock over a bond, with no guarantee of ever getting your money back, this requirement will at least keep you from taking too much of a gamble with your hard-earned cash.

Valuation Approaches

There are basically two approaches for common stock valuation: top-down and bottom-up. Under either of the two fundamental approaches, an investor will have to work with individual company data. In reality, each of these approaches is used by investors and security analysts when doing fundamental analysis. With the bottom-up approach, investors focus directly on a company's prospects. Analysis of such information as the company's products, its competitive position, and its financial status leads to an estimate of the company's earnings potential and, ultimately, its value in the market. Considerable time and effort are required to produce the type of detailed financial analysis needed to understand a firm's standing. The emphasis in this approach is on finding companies with good long-term growth prospects and making accurate earnings estimates.

The top-down approach is the opposite of the bottom-up approach. Investors begin with the economy and the overall market, considering such important factors as interest rates and inflation. They next consider likely industry prospects, or sectors of the economy that are likely to do particularly well (or particularly poorly). Finally, having decided that factors are favorable for investing and having determined which parts of the overall economy are likely to perform well, investors should proceed to analyze individual companies.

I believe that both approaches add value. However, since our recommendation is that investors primarily concentrate on four sectors of the economy, a top-down approach is less relevant. Therefore, this chapter will concentrate on the bottom-up approach. To organize this effort, bottom-up fundamental research is often broken into two categories: growth investing and value investing.

Growth Stocks—Catching the Momentum

The growth style of investing focuses on companies with strong earnings and accelerating capital growth. A growth investor will make investment decisions based on forecasts of continuing growth in earnings. Growth investing emphasizes qualitative criteria, including value judgments about the company, its markets, its management, and its ability to extract future earnings growth from the particular industry. Quantitative indicators of interest to the growth investor include high price/earnings ratios, high price/sales ratios, and low dividend yields.

A high P/E ratio suggests that the market is prepared to pay more per share in anticipation of future earnings. A low dividend yield suggests that the company is reinvesting rather than distributing profits. These indicators are considered in relation to the company's immediate competitors. The companies with the highest P/E ratios relative to their industry will often be dominant within their market segment and have strong growth prospects. Growth investors generally focus on premium and leading-edge companies.

Some industry sectors by their nature have stronger growth characteristics, particularly more innovative and speculative industries. For example, during the bull run on the U.S. stock markets during the late 1990s, the technology sector was a major area of growth investment. On observing strong earnings growth, a growth investor will decide whether to buy shares based on whether the company's growth will continue at its present rate and whether it will increase or decrease. If it is expected to increase, the growth investor will consider it a candidate for purchase.

The key research question is, At what point will the company's growth flatten out or fall? If a company's growth rate slows or reverses, it is no longer attractive to a growth investor. Growth investors are normally prepared to pay a premium for what they believe to be high-quality shares. The potential downside in growth investing is that if a company goes into sudden decline and the share price falls, the investor can lose capital value rapidly.

Growth stocks carry high expectations of above-average future growth in earnings and above-average valuations. Investors expect these stocks to perform well in the future and are willing to pay high P/E multiples for this expected growth. The danger is that the price may become too high. Generally, once a company sports a P/E ratio above 50, the risk significantly escalates. Many technology growth stocks traded at a P/E ratio of above 100 during 1999. This is unsustainable. No company in the history of the stock market has been able to maintain such a high P/E level for a sustained period of time.

Value Stocks—Looking for Bargains

The bargain-hunting value style involves looking for shares that are underpriced in relation to the company's future potential. A value investor will invest in a company in the expectation that its shares will increase in value over time. Value investing is based essentially on quantitative criteria: asset values, cash flow, and discounted future earnings. The key properties of value shares are low price/earnings and price/sales ratios and normally higher dividend yields. On observing a company's earnings growth, a value manager will decide whether to buy shares based on the company's consistency or recovery prospects. The key research questions are (1) Does the current P/E ratio warrant an investment in a slow-growth company? and (2) Is the company a higher growth candidate that has dropped in price due to a temporary problem? If this is the case, will the company's earnings growth recover, and if so, when? The key to value investing is to find bargain shares (priced low historically or for temporary and/or irrational reasons), avoiding shares that are merely cheap (priced low because the company is failing).

The buying opportunity is identified when a company undergoing some immediate problems is perceived to have good chances of recovery in the medium to long term. If there is a loss in market confidence in the company, the share price may fall, and the value investor can step in. Once the share price has achieved a suitable value, reflecting the predicted turnaround in company performance, the shareholding is sold, realizing a capital gain. A potential risk in value investing is that the company may not turn around, in which case the share price may stay static or fall.

Performance of Growth and Value Stocks

Although many academics argue that value stocks outperform growth stocks, the returns for individuals investing through mutual funds demonstrate a near match. A 2005 study "Do Investors Capture the Value Premium?," written by Todd Houge at The University of Iowa and Tim Loughran at The University of Notre Dame, found that large-company mutual funds in both the value and growth styles returned just over 11% for the period 1975–2002. This paper contradicted many studies demonstrating that owning value stocks offers better long-term performance than growth stocks. These studies, led by Eugene Fama and Kenneth French, established the current consensus that the value style of investing does indeed offer a return premium. There are several theories as to why this has been the case, among the most persuasive being a series of behavioral arguments put forth by leading researchers. These studies suggest that the outperformance of value stocks may result from investors' tendency toward common behavioral traits, including the belief that the future will be similar to the past, overreaction to unexpected events, "herding" behavior that leads at times to overemphasis of a particular style or sector, overconfidence, and aversion to regret. All of these behaviors can cause price anomalies that create buying opportunities for value investors.

Another key ingredient argued for value outperformance is lower business appraisals. Value stocks are plainly confined to a P/E range, whereas growth stocks have an upper limit that is infinite. When growth stocks reach a high plateau in regard to P/E ratios, the ensuing returns are generally much lower than the category average over time. In addition, growth stocks tend to lose more in bear markets. In the last two major bear markets, growth stocks fared far worse than value stocks. From January 1973 until late 1974, large-growth stocks lost 45% of their value, while large-value stocks lost 26%. Similarly, from April 2000 to September 2002, large-growth stocks lost 46% versus only 27% for large-value stocks. These losses, academics insist, dramatically reduce the long-term investment returns of growth stocks.

However, the recent study by Houge and Loughran reasoned that although a premium may exist, investors have not been able to capture the excess return through mutual funds. The study also maintained that any potential value premium is generated outside the securities held by most mutual funds.

TABLE 9.1 Annualized Returns and Standard Deviations for Return
Data: January 1975–December 2002

Index	Return	SD
S&P 500	11.53%	14.88
Large Growth Funds	11.30%	16.65
Large Value Funds	11.41%	15.39

Source: Hough/Loughran Study.

Simply put, being growth or value oriented had no material impact on a mutual fund's performance. Listed in Table 9.1 are the annualized returns and standard deviations for return data from January 1975 through December 2002.

The Hough/Loughran study also found that the returns by style also varied over time. From 1965 to 1983, a period widely known to favor the value style, large-value funds averaged a 9.92% annual return, compared with 8.73% for large-growth funds. This performance differential reverses over 1984–2001, as large-growth funds generated a 14.1% average return compared with 12.9% for large value funds. Thus, one style can outperform in any time period. However, although the long-term returns are nearly identical, large differences between value and growth returns happen over time. This is especially the case over the past 10 years as growth and value have had extraordinary return differences, sometimes over 30 percentage points of underperformance. Table 9.2 indicates the return differential between the value and growth styles since 1992.

Between the third quarter of 1994 and the second quarter of 2000, the S&P Growth Index produced annualized total returns of 30%, versus only about 18% for the S&P Value Index. Since 2000, value has turned the tables and dramatically outperformed growth. Growth has outperformed value in only two of the past eight years. Since the two styles are successful at different times, combining them in one portfolio can create a buffer against

TABLE 9.2 Return Differential Between Value and Growth Styles Since 1992

Year	Growth	Value
1992	5.1%	10.5%
1993	1.7%	18.6%
1994	3.1%	−0.6%
1995	38.1%	37.1%
1996	24.0%	22.0%
1997	36.5%	30.6%
1998	42.2%	14.7%
1999	28.2%	3.2%
2000	−22.1%	6.1%
2001	−26.7%	7.1%
2002	−25.2%	−20.5%
2003	28.2%	27.7%
2004	6.3%	16.5%
2005	3.6%	6.1%
2006	10.8%	20.6%
2007	8.8%	1.5%
2008	−34.9%	−39.2%
2009	39.6%	26.3%
2010	17.1%	16.3%

Source: Standard & Poor's.

dramatic swings, reducing volatility and the subsequent drag on returns. In our analysis, the surest way to maximize the benefits of style investing is to combine growth and value in a single portfolio, maintaining the proportions evenly in a 50/50 split through regular rebalancing. Research from Bernstein and Vanguard shows that since 1980, a 50/50 portfolio beats the market by nearly 2% per year. Given that both styles have nearly equal performance and either style can outperform for a significant time period, I recommend a blending of styles. Rather than attempt to second-guess the market by switching in and out of

TABLE 9.3 U.S. Sector Concentration

Sector	Value	Growth
Industrials	49	51
Consumer Discretionary	11	89
Energy	94	6
Finance	90	10
Health Care	35	65
Consumer Staples	69	31
Materials	65	35
Services	41	59
Technology	8	92

Source: HSBC, number of stocks in value/growth portfolio as a percentage of the total number of stocks within that sector 2009.

styles as they roll with the cycle, it is prudent to maintain an equal balance in your investment between the two. Fortunately, my recommended sectors—health care, staples, financials, technology, and energy—all offer both value and growth candidates. This is by design. A portfolio composed of stocks from these five sectors will naturally be well diversified between the two investment styles (see Table 9.3).

As this table demonstrates, the technology and health care sectors are primarily in the growth category, whereas the financial, staples, and energy sectors fall primarily into the value camp.

Importance of Dividends

As mentioned in Chapter 1, dividends are of critical importance, accounting for 43 percent of the S&P 500s return since 1930. Dividend yield should be an important consideration in seeking out attractive stock candidates, whether growth or value. There is a plethora of academic research which concludes that portfolios consisting of higher than average yielding stocks produce returns that are more attractive relative to lower yielding stocks.

In the same publication that demonstrated the superior perform-ance of our favored sectors, *The Future for Investors*, Professor Jeremy Siegel inspected the performance of the constituent stocks of the S&P 500 Stock Index ordered by dividend yield from 1957 to 2002. The highest yielding top 20% of S&P 500 in-dex based on yield produced an annualized return of 14.2% ver-sus an annualized return of 11.1% for the S&P 500 Index. Other more recent studies have confirmed Dr. Siegel's results. A 2008 study by Northern Trust[1] looked at dividend yield and overall performance of the largest 750 U.S. stocks over forty years. Stocks with above-average dividend yields outperformed those with below-average yields by 2.0% over a 1-year holding period, 6.3% over a 3-year holding period, and 9.8% over a 5-year hold-ing period. Much of the outperformance not only comes from the added income component that high dividend stocks main-tain, but also the strong defensive capability of these stocks. According to S&P 500 Index data from 1930 to 2008, stocks de-cline an average of −13.6% in falling markets. However, during these same time periods, dividends return an average of +4.5%—offsetting about one third of market losses. The stability of dividend paying stocks is no doubt due to the ability of the firm to pay out a significant percentage of net income in divi-dends, rain or shine. I recommend that a large percentage of your stock portfolio be devoted to firms that pay dividends. It will provide an additional safety net and added income during poor market cycles like 2008/2009.

Intrinsic and Relative Valuation

There is a further bifurcation within the valuation process. Two additional methods for evaluating the stock price of a company are available: absolute valuation and relative valuation. Absolute valuation models, such as the dividend discount or discounted cash flow models, rely on data from the given firm followed by a forecast of future streams of earnings, dividends, or cash. In regard to absolute models, the discounted cash flow method is the most popular. Money managers and academics have been using it for decades, coming up with numerous variations: the dividend–discount model (best suited for companies paying dividends) and the discounted cash flow to the firm model (DCF) being the most popular. Investment bankers also use these models to price companies involved in mergers or acquisitions.

These models, with their various permutations, represent an attempt to do the same two things: The first is to look at factors such as growth rates and profit margins to project how much money a company can generate in the future; the second is to discount the future cash flows back to today's dollars. The difficulty in these models is the substantial differences that result by making only small changes in the inputs. While this method is philosophically correct, it is a very impractical model. Therefore, I recommend a relative value approach to stock valuation. Relative valuation models use the previously mentioned ratios, such as P/E, P/S, PEG, and so forth.

Relative value seeks to determine the true value of a stock by comparing these multiples to those of the overall market, similar firms, or the company's own history. For example, if two companies participate in the same industry, with comparable balance sheets and income statements and equal growth rates, their P/Es should be very similar. If their P/Es are different, an analyst must investigate why such a discrepancy exists. Each company also has a trading history. Stocks will trade either below, equal to, or above their own historical valuation. Finding stocks that trade at a low historical valuation can offer an investor substantial rewards. In the previous chapters on the sectors, I have given you several case studies that use fundamental valuation techniques.

CHAPTER 10

The Selection Process

Do not hire a man who does your work for money, but him who does it for the love of it.

Henry David Thoreau

To be a successful stock investor, an individual must follow a disciplined approach. There are literally thousands of publicly traded companies. No investor can examine them all. Fortunately, through focusing on the five major sectors of the economy, the list of potential investments is dramatically reduced. In fact, I recommend that you limit your buy list to about 300 publicly traded companies (see sector chapters). Within these 300 firms, you will find plenty of attractive candidates. The following criteria should be used:

Diversify across the Major Recommended Sectors

- Select 10 to 12 health care stocks.
- Select 8 to 10 consumer staples stocks.
- Select 8 to 10 energy stocks.
- Select 4 to 6 technology stocks.
- Select 4 to 6 financial stocks.
- Select 2 to 5 stocks in other sectors with a high safety rating.
- Select companies of a large size (5 billion market cap >).

- Select companies that are leaders in their field and possess a strong financial position as rated by Standard & Poor's.
- Select companies that are No. 1 or No. 2 within their respective industry in market share, debt levels, profitability, and FCF yield.
- Select companies that have a P/E or P/S ratio below their 5-year average.
- Select companies that possess a PEG ratio less than 1.5 (for health care, energy, staples, and financial stocks) and less than 2 (for technology stocks).

The portfolio of 35 stocks that you maintain will show a balance of value and growth. Because the financial and energy sectors primarily contain value stocks, your overall average P/E ratio should be reasonably low. My recommendation is to immediately build a portfolio from the primary sectors. The principal emphasis should be on industry leaders. Once your portfolio is built, just a little pruning will be necessary. You don't need to follow your companies like a hawk. Just ensure that you examine the fundamentals closely from time to time. Pay close attention to the P/E and P/S of your particular company. If the P/E or P/S climbs quite above the long-term average, you should take a good hard look at the firm's merits. Watch for trends in the financial ratios discussed in Chapter 9. If the financial ratios deteriorate considerably, selling your position is most likely warranted.

My primary buy strategy is to add stocks to the portfolio when the stocks in the recommended sectors are out of favor. Being a contrarian investor is quite difficult, but it is the most profitable trading strategy for the buy-and-hold investor. In the field of finance, contrarian investment strategies go against what is known as the efficient-market hypothesis (EMH). The theory asserts that the financial markets are "informationally efficient"—that is, one cannot consistently realize returns in excess of standard market return on a consistent basis. This is because the information about individual firms and the markets is publicly available at the time the investment is made. The efficient-market hypothesis was developed by Professor Eugene Fama at the University of Chicago. It was widely accepted up until the 1980s, when behavior finance economists, who had been a periphery component in academic circles, came out with several studies that poked holes in the EMH.

For a review, there are three major versions of the hypothesis: weak, semi-strong, and strong. The weak EMH theory claims that prices on any security already reflect all historic publicly available information. The semi-strong EMH theory claims both that prices reflect all publicly available information and that prices instantly transform to reflect new public information. The strong EMH theory additionally claims that prices instantly reflect even secret or insider information. There is evidence for and against the weak and semi-strong EMHs, while there is now commanding proof against strong EMH.

Various academic studies over the past 20 years have pointed out signs of inefficiency in financial markets. The EMH encountered its first heavy assault from Werner DeBondt and Richard Thaler (1985).[1] In their prominent study, it was found that returns in U.S. stocks exhibit a unique anomaly, or as cited afterward, an overreaction. The overreaction behavior found in their study was that previous loser stocks tended to become winners, while previous winners tend to become losers over time. DeBondt and Thaler were among the initial researchers to propose the probability of earning contrarian profits by taking advantage of the price-reversal phenomenon. They noted that in using 3- to 5-year data, contrarian strategies, which involve buying past losers and selling past winners, yield statistically significant positive profits as high as nearly 8% per year across the holding period. Their study was followed by additional academic papers. Over time a mounting body of literature confirmed this overreaction hypothesis. Gishan Dissanaike at Cambridge also found compelling verification of overreaction and positive profits of contrarian strategy for UK markets.[2] Similar results have been found in the Japanese, Indian, Canadian, and Australian markets.

Contrarian strategies that propose buying past losers and selling past winners are now known as the winners and losers effect. DeBondt and Thaler concluded that the reason for the subsequent outperformance is that stock investors overreact to bad news. Investors are subject to waves of optimism and pessimism that cause prices to deviate systematically from their fundamental values. This overreaction on the negative side drives down the stock price below an intrinsic level. Once the overreaction subsides, the stock can outperform, but only over a longer time frame. A longer time frame is a critical component to the success of the strategy. The time period used in the studies has generally been three to five years.

As we have previously detailed, the five major recommended sectors all possess low correlations to each other. This means that generally one sector (or at least one sub-sector) will be out of favor at any given time. This will give a contrarian investor looking for "losers" plenty of investment opportunities at any given time. Please see the stock case studies at the end of Chapters 3–7 for specific examples of contrarian investing.

In regard to selling a stock, I generally will liquidate a position when one or more of the following conditions have been met:

- The company failed to meet earnings expectations for two consecutive quarters.
- The company price/earnings (PE) ratio climbed well above the historical average.
- Financial ratios have deteriorated.
- Free cash flow yield dropped below 4%.
- Any accounting irregularities have been disclosed.

Smaller Accounts

Unless you have at least $30,000 to invest, you should not invest directly in stocks. Instead, I recommend that you use funds to follow my investment strategy. The reason is simple—high costs. To be adequately diversified, you must own at least 35 stocks. Owning fewer stocks subjects you to additional risks for which you are generally not compensated. Owning less than 35 stocks will also prevent you from properly covering all the four recommended major sectors. The inherent problem with small accounts is that commissions and fees eat into your return. For example, say you attempt to maintain a 35-stock portfolio with only a $10,000 account.

To get your portfolio started (even if your account is held at a deep-discount broker such as Ameritrade), initial cost would be 35 stocks × $10.99 a trade, or $384.65. If turnover in the portfolio averaged 25 percent (or you sold and replaced a stock seven times), additional commissions would amount to $153.86. Therefore, your total first-year trading costs would amount to $538.51, or 5.3 percent of your portfolio. Of course, after the first year, your trading fees would be reduced to 1.5 percent of your portfolio. However, that amount is still too dear. You should attempt to keep your trading costs to less than 0.5% of your portfolio over time. Therefore, a $30,000 minimum requirement is quite prudent.

Once you have built up $30,000 in funds, you can begin to gravitate towards individual stocks. At the time you reach this dollar amount, it is fine to add to your portfolio one stock at a time. This is because you are still diversified by virtue of having most of your money in mutual funds. Merely limit yourself to investing no more than 3% of your money, to start, in any one stock. Gradually move out of funds and into stocks over time.

ETFs

There are several fund alternatives you can choose from, including regular mutual funds, closed-end funds, and ETFs. ETFs offer one of the most effective strategies. The acronym ETF stands for exchange traded funds. Unknown to most investors, they've actually been around for years. As giant asset managers such as Barclays Global Investors and State Street have rolled out scores of new offerings in recent years, ETFs have once again taken the limelight. At the most basic level, ETFs are just what their name implies—baskets of securities that are traded, like individual stocks, on an exchange (most offerings currently trade on the American Stock Exchange). There are several advantages of ETFs:

Trading flexibility

One key advantage that ETFs have over traditional mutual funds is trading flexibility. ETFs trade throughout the day, so you can buy and sell them when you want. Simply put, ETFs diversify an investment like funds but trade like stocks.

Costs

In terms of the annual expenses charged to investors, ETFs are considerably less expensive than the vast majority of mutual funds. Annual expense ratios for the largest ETFs (Ishares) range from 0.09 percent for iShares S&P 500 Index, to 0.99 percent for several of the iShares MSCI offerings.

Taxes

With a regular mutual fund, investor selling can force managers to sell stocks in order to meet redemptions, which can result in taxable capital-gains distributions being paid to shareholders. In contrast, most trading in ETFs takes place between shareholders, shielding the fund from any need to sell stocks to meet redemptions. Furthermore, redemptions made by large investors are paid in kind, again protecting shareholders from taxable events. All of this should make ETFs more tax-efficient than most mutual funds, and they may therefore hold a special attraction for investors in taxable accounts. Keep in mind, however, that ETFs can and do make capital-gains distributions, inasmuch as they must still buy and sell stocks to adjust for changes to their underlying benchmarks.

Performance

ETFs are index funds. This means the fund owns a sampling of investments in its respective category and does not try to select one company over another. ETFs offer an excellent choice of investments. All my recommended sectors are available in ETFs. The five following ETF investments offer global diversification, which I recommend:

- S&P Global Healthcare Sector Fund (Symbol: IXJ)
- S&P Global Consumer Staples Sector Fund (Symbol: KXI)
- S&P Global Financial Sector Fund (Symbol: IXG)
- S&P Global Technology Sector Fund (Symbol: IXN)
- S&P Global Energy Sector Fund (Symbol: IXC)

With five purchases, you can gain diversified exposure to all my sectors. In sum, ETFs are very low-cost investment products that deliver the diversification of mutual funds with the tradability of individual stocks. That is an exceptional package of qualities, which explains why ETFs continue to grow in assets and breadth of product even through this bear market.

MUTUAL FUNDS   ETFs have several advantages over traditional mutual funds and offer a low-cost method to invest in the four recommended sectors. However, if you want to have an active manager select the stocks as opposed to the index strategy that ETFs practice, there are several excellent alternatives within mutual fund families. Choosing a sector mutual fund in combination with ETFs can also provide enhanced diversification. There are two criteria you need to consider before choosing a mutual fund.

Never choose a mutual fund that has a sales charge, called a load, or one with a continuous load called a 12b-1 charge. These charges are detailed in the beginning of the prospectus that you must receive in order to invest in any fund. Academic studies have shown that there is no performance difference between a fund that charges a load and a no-load fund. A load is purely an additional cost that provides you no added benefit. As with ETFs, choose a fund that has both a low expense ratio and a low portfolio turnover rate.

I recommend the following active funds for each sector category:

Health Care: Vanguard Health Care Fund (Symbol: VGHCX)

This is the best health care fund on the market today. With more than 18 years under his belt, manager Ed Owens has proved to be quite adept at choosing health care stocks. His fund continually ranks in the top percentage of health care funds. Its 18% annual return since 1992 is at the top of the list. The fund's volatility is also very low, and its expense ratio is a minuscule 0.31%. Mr. Owens also follows a relative-value approach, choosing stocks in much the same manner as I recommend in Chapter 11. Runner-up: Fidelity Select Health Care (FSPHX).

Staples: Fidelity Consumer Staples Fund (Symbol: FDFAX)

This is a solid fund that is also the longest running in its category. Manager Bob Lee has been willing to stray from his benchmark, but he also holds the biggest staples firms. These large firms have fared best over the past year. He also uses smaller names. These firms may not have the same size or geographic reach, but Lee argues they have the same defensive characteristics as bigger players. Lee's experience argues for giving this fund the nod over an ETF as your primary staples exposure. Runner-up: ICON Leisure & Consumer Staples (ICLEX).

Financials: T. Rowe Price Financial Fund (Symbol: PSIRX)

Over its 15-year life, the fund has put up strong results. It consistently outperforms other funds within its category. Despite having three different managers during the stretch, the fund has consistently cranked out solid returns. Moreover, the fund has a deep bench with a solid cadre of junior analysts. The fund is well diversified across the different financials' sub-sectors and maintains a relatively small asset base (which allows flexibility). This financial fund typically holds companies with strong management, above-average earnings-growth rates, and strong market share. Turnover is also very low. The fund outperformed 80% of its category during the 2008 financial stock meltdown. The expense ratio, at 0.91%, is very reasonable and below the category average. Runner-up: John Hancock Financial Industries Fund (FIDIX).

Technology: Northern Technology Fund (Symbol: NTCHX)

Compared with its tech-fund peers, this fund has done an excellent job. It maintains a strong five-year track record, beating over 80% of its peers in total return. The fund is managed by John Leo and George Gilbert. Both are very experienced and have been with the fund since inception in 1996. Their portfolio is generally defensively positioned and concentrates on technology blue-chips. They tend to focus on buying companies with strong competitive positions that are gaining market share within their sub-sector. Large-cap companies are the primary focus. The expense ratio of the fund is a little high at 1.25%, but still below the category average. Runner-up: Dreyfus Premier Technology Fund (DGVRX).

Energy: Vanguard Energy Fund (Symbol: VGENX)

Another Vanguard offering, this energy fund maintains stakes throughout the energy sector, making it one of the most diversified funds available. The fund has been led by long-time manager Ernst von Metzsch since 1984. Von Metzsch has a contrarian style, buying large-cap stocks that are out of favor. A sizeable portion of this energy fund is also earmarked for foreign stocks, giving it added diversification. Volatility is generally tame in that the fund maintains a high exposure to major oil companies. As a Vanguard offering, its expense ratio is the lowest in the category, at 0.39%. With a sagacious investment strategy and low costs, this fund stands out among energy funds. Runner-up: Excelsior Energy & Nat Resources Fund (UMESX).

REITS, PRECIOUS METALS, AND BOND FUNDS   For smaller investors, excellent alternatives within ETFs and mutual funds are also available for the recommended alternative components: real estate investment trusts, corporate bonds, and precious metals. We are avoiding a strict commodity fund, because we will instead use its components.

For REITs I recommend:

Fidelity Real Estate Investment (Symbol: FRESX)

This fund has the largest assets in its respective category with a solid management team and low expense ratio. Manager Steve Buller prefers large, liquid companies and keeps the fund very diversified across all categories. This fund also tends to favor real estate investment trusts (REITs) over real estate operating companies (REOCs). It has been one of the top-performing funds in its category over the past five years. Runner-up: Morgan Stanley US Real Estate Fund (MSUSX).

For bonds I recommend:

Prudential Short-Term Corporate Fund (Symbol: PBSMX)

This fund generally offers a higher-than-average yield and also provides good downside protection when credit markets are poor. The fund has never lost money during any two-year rolling period since the existing management team was hired more than a decade ago. The fund has also posted strong long-term results, with 3-, 5- and 10-year returns through the end of March 2011 that outperform 90% of the peer group. Runner-up: Oppenheimer Corporate Bond Fund (OFIAX).

For commodities I recommend:

Vanguard Precious Metals & Mining Fund (Symbol: VGPMX)

Fund manager Graham French has delivered strong returns without taking on as much risk as some peers. Indeed, the fund has been less volatile (when measured by standard deviation) than its average fund peer over the long term. French's strategy, which involves investing across a broad spectrum of metals and mining stocks, can limit gains when one particular commodity is booming, but also pads the fund during downturns. French also prefers to invest in established companies with healthy financial statements; he tends to avoid companies that don't have producing mines yet. The fund is also the cheapest offering in its category by a long shot. Its expense ratio is even lower than that of the gold exchange-traded fund, which are other ways to get exposure to the yellow metal. Runner-up: AIM Precious Metals Fund (IGDAX).

CHAPTER 11

The Right Allocation

The further backward you look, the further ahead you can see.

Winston Churchill

The goal of asset allocation is to obtain a proportional relationship among the various asset classes that will maximize returns and minimize risk, while taking into account your individual situation and goals. Proper asset allocation, according to most experts, will help you reduce risk while minimizing the impact of a capital loss.

Today, everyone is on the asset allocation bandwagon. This includes legions of financial planners, mutual fund companies, 401(k) sponsors, and the media. Asset allocation blueprints are now routinely published in major newspapers and magazines. The writers all profess how great these plans are and how they can help you secure a sound financial future. But there are several problems with the typical recommended financial plans that have been pointed out throughout this text:

- Bonds do reduce risk, but they also reduce returns. Bonds have provided only a marginal return above inflation over the past 60 years.

- Adding international stocks can be beneficial for diversification, but only if the sectors added to the portfolio are different from the current sector weights within that portfolio.

Using a sector-focused strategy alongside recommendations for additional asset classes can offer an investor a path to better returns. Listed in the following sections are three model portfolios based on the tenets of this book. I recommend only three model portfolios. This is because either one of these three models should meet your needs, whether you are 25 or 65 years of age. The following sections present the models and the characteristics of a comfortable owner.

Aggressive Portfolio

85% Stocks, 10% Bonds/REITs, 5% Precious Metals

This portfolio maintains the highest concentration in stocks. If you are below age 40 and can embrace a very high level of volatility, my aggressive model portfolio should be suitable for you. Conditions include
- High return expectations for your investments.
- Ability to tolerate higher degrees of fluctuation (sharp, short-term volatility).
- Being in the wealth-accumulation stage of life.
- Having 20 years or more before you will need to use the money for your retirement.

Recommended Aggressive Asset Allocation

- 30% health care stocks
- 30% consumer staples stocks
- 15% energy stocks
- 7.5% technology stocks

- 2.5% financial stocks
- 5% BB- to BBB-rated corporate bonds
- 5% REITs
- 5% precious metals

Moderate Portfolio

70% Stocks, 25% Bonds/REITs, 5% Precious Metals

This portfolio maintains a higher concentration in stocks. If you are below age 55 and can embrace a higher level of volatility, my aggressive model portfolio should be suitable for you. Conditions include

- Moderately high return expectations for your investments.
- Ability to tolerate moderately high degrees of fluctuation (sharp, short-term volatility).
- Being in the wealth-accumulation stage of life.
- Having 10 years or more before you will need to use the money for your retirement.

Recommended Moderate Asset Allocation

- 25% health care stocks
- 25% consumer staples stocks
- 10% energy stocks
- 7.5% technology stocks
- 2.5% financial stocks
- 20% BB- to BBB-rated corporate bonds
- 5% REITs
- 5% precious metals

For investors at age 55 or older, I recommend a more conservative approach.

Balanced Portfolio

55% Stocks, 40% Bonds/REITs, 5% Precious Metals

This intermediate-risk portfolio provides a blend of equities and income-oriented investments. Conditions include

- Having moderate return expectations for your investments.
- Wanting some current income return on your investments.
- Being willing and able to accept a moderate level of risk and return.
- Being in retirement or approaching retirement.
- Being concerned that the impact of inflation may erode the value of your investments.

Now if you are a retiree, you might scoff at my recommendation of putting only 35% of your assets in bonds. In my mind, retirees have always put too much emphasis on bonds—ignoring stocks. This, too, can be a mistake. Remember that you could spend 20, 30, or more years in retirement, so you'll want stocks to help provide investment growth potential and hedge against inflation. This is especially true if you retire early, which many Americans are doing today. But even if you retire at the customary age of 65, statistics are still daunting. According to the census bureau, a 65-year-old has a 40% chance of living to age 90. If both a husband and wife are 65, there is almost an 80% chance one of you will live to age 90. And, that is not to say that you could not live to age 100. If so, that would be 30 years that your retirement portfolio would have to keep growing.

Therefore, you will also want to maintain a diversified portfolio primarily based on stocks. Here is the balanced portfolio recommendation:

Recommended Balanced Asset Allocation

- 20% health care stocks
- 20% consumer staples stocks
- 10% energy stocks
- 5% technology stocks
- 35% BB- to BBB-rated corporate bonds
- 5% REITs
- 5% precious metals

How do the three model portfolios stand up over the long-term? Actually, very well. The return on the aggressive portfolio outperforms the S&P 500 Index by 1.5% per year. The moderate portfolio, despite the addition of bonds, also outperforms the S&P 500 Index nearly as well with less risk. The balanced portfolio, despite its heavy corporate bond weight, outperforms a similarly weighted balanced portfolio. The recommended portfolios also fare very well in poor markets. During the 24-year period ending in 2010, the aggressive portfolio had only three negative years (2001, 2002, 2008) versus the S&P 500's five (1990, 2000, 2001, 2002, 2008). Additionally, each of the declines was substantially less than those of the stock index (see Table 11.1).

Risk, as measured by standard deviation, is also reduced greatly for both the aggressive and balanced portfolios. The standard deviations of the aggressive and balanced portfolios were 12.65 and 10.79, respectively. This compares favorably with the S&P 500, which maintained a standard deviation of 16.05. This strengthens the argument that my preferred sectors and income components are not well correlated and provide excellent diversification. In the last bear stock market, the drop in 2008 in the recommended aggressive portfolio was more than 10% better than that of the stock index. The recommended balanced portfolio, despite its heavy weight in riskier corporate

TABLE 11.1 Portfolio Returns 1986–2010*

Portfolio	Annualized Return 1986–2010
Aggressive Portfolio	11.94%
Moderate Portfolio	11.73%
Balanced Portfolio	11.51%
S&P 500 Index	10.36%
50% S&P 500 Index/	
50% U.S. Treasuries	9.34%

Source: Lipper Inc; A Reuters Company, 1986–1998, Lipper Data, Financials measured by Financial Services Funds, consumer staples by Fidelity Consumer Staples Fund, health care by Healthcare/Biotechnology funds, energy by Natural Resources Funds, and technology by Science and Technology Funds. Return data from 1999–2008, SPDR Sector ETFs. REIT returns from the NAREIT index. Precious metals returns from Morningstar. Corporate bond data from Credit Suisse. U.S. Treasury bonds, from Ibbottson.
*Data through December 31, 2010.

bonds, fared even better. It incurred a loss in only one year since 1986, whereas the traditional allocated portfolios had four losing years.

Listed in Table 11.2 are the annual returns for the S&P 500 Index, and my two more aggressive model portfolios, presented year by year.

Listed in Table 11.3 is the annual return for the recommended balanced portfolio versus a 50/50 mix of the S&P 500 Index and intermediate Treasury bonds.

Table 11.4 lists my five recommended stock sectors and the annual returns based on Lipper Mutual Fund (1986–1998) and SPDR ETFs (1999–2010) data.

Table 11.5 shows the four alternative investment components and the annual returns.

These results prove that a new "sector" asset allocation combined with favoring corporate bonds is a key element of a successful investment strategy. The implication of these results is

TABLE 11.2 Annual Returns for the S&P 500 Index with Aggressive Model Portfolios*

Year	Aggressive	Moderate	S&P 500
1986	16.48%	17.79%	18.67%
1987	4.89%	5.38%	5.25%
1988	16.54%	16.31%	16.61%
1989	38.14%	31.17%	31.69%
1990	8.40%	6.00%	−3.11%
1991	38.43%	37.88%	30.47%
1992	0.24%	4.47%	7.62%
1993	9.75%	10.82%	10.08%
1994	3.27%	3.03%	1.32%
1995	35.09%	32.75%	37.58%
1996	19.94%	17.78%	22.96%
1997	17.78%	17.69%	33.36%
1998	8.53%	10.12%	28.58%
1999	11.92%	10.97%	21.04%
2000	8.92%	6.66%	−9.11%
2001	−6.78%	−2.88%	−11.89%
2002	−7.90%	−5.94%	−22.10%
2003	20.72%	21.64%	28.58%
2004	11.26%	9.58%	10.88%
2005	13.53%	9.39%	4.83%
2006	14.68%	13.66%	15.80%
2007	14.88%	10.38%	5.54%
2008	−25.08%	−24.35%	−36.99%
2009	22.19%	25.51%	26.46%
2010	12.45%	14.03%	15.06%
Annual Return	**11.94%**	**11.73%**	**10.36%**

Source: Lipper Inc; A Reuters Company, 1986–1998, Lipper Data, financials measured by Financial Services Funds, consumer staples by Fidelity Consumer Staples Fund, health care by Healthcare/Biotechnology funds, energy by Natural Resources Funds, and technology by Science and Technology Funds. Return data from 1999–2008, SPDR Sector ETFs. REIT returns from the NAREIT index. Precious metals returns from Morningstar. Corporate bond data from Credit Suisse. U.S. Treasury bonds, from Ibbottson.

*Data through December 31, 2010.

TABLE 11.3 Annual Return for the Recommended Balanced Portfolio versus a 50/50 Mix of the S&P 500 Index and Intermediate Treasury Bonds*

Year	Recommended Balanced	50% S&P 500 50% Treasury
1986	18.41%	15.87%
1987	6.09%	4.43%
1988	15.76%	11.51%
1989	27.23%	22.19%
1990	4.69%	3.23%
1991	34.11%	22.29%
1992	5.40%	7.28%
1993	11.43%	9.13%
1994	2.14%	−0.22%
1995	29.52%	26.00%
1996	16.74%	13.51%
1997	15.51%	20.54%
1998	8.01%	18.54%
1999	9.31%	10.77%
2000	6.93%	0.68%
2001	0.20%	−1.74%
2002	−3.04%	−6.23%
2003	21.48%	15.44%
2004	10.09%	6.61%
2005	9.17%	3.26%
2006	12.92%	9.82%
2007	9.92%	5.12%
2008	−22.62%	−12.57%
2009	27.19%	16.20%
2010	14.68%	10.80%
Annual Return	11.51%	9.34%

Source: Lipper Inc; A Reuters Company, 1986–1998, Lipper Data, financials measured by Financial Services Funds, consumer staples by Fidelity Consumer Staples Fund, health care by Healthcare/Biotechnology funds, energy by Natural Resources Funds, and technology by Science and Technology Funds. Return data from 1999–2008, SPDR Sector ETFs. REIT returns from the NAREIT index. Precious metals returns from Morningstar. Corporate bond data from Credit Suisse. U.S. Treasury bonds, from Ibbottson.

*Data through December 31, 2010.

TABLE 11.4 Five Recommended Stock Sectors and the Annual Returns Based on Lipper Mutual Fund (1986–1998) and SPDR ETFs (1999–2010) Data*

Year	Health Care	Staples	Energy	Tech	Financials
1986	16.60%	22.50%	10.68%	6.44%	15.13%
1987	−1.16%	7.51%	9.18%	4.05%	−11.17%
1988	12.35%	26.77%	9.36%	4.87%	19.26%
1989	46.33%	38.88%	34.31%	20.70%	24.00%
1990	20.19%	12.90%	−6.80%	0.87%	−15.91%
1991	68.41%	34.09%	1.35%	50.18%	58.44%
1992	−6.65%	2.03%	1.48%	14.31%	34.96%
1993	3.03%	8.82%	21.99%	25.58%	15.67%
1994	2.62%	6.09%	−2.92%	13.67%	−2.68%
1995	46.15%	36.64%	20.22%	42.52%	41.88%
1996	13.07%	13.35%	34.42%	20.44%	28.72%
1997	21.07%	30.34%	2.41%	10.21%	45.82%
1998	18.83%	15.69%	−23.57%	52.04%	6.35%
1999	20.90%	−14.49%	19.04%	66.69%	3.57%
2000	−11.63%	26.04%	24.92%	−42.04%	25.93%
2001	0.04%	−9.63%	−18.04%	−22.76%	−8.90%
2002	−1.44%	−19.78%	−14.56%	−38.28%	−14.65%
2003	15.14%	11.26%	26.76%	39.49%	31.01%
2004	1.73%	8.11%	33.88%	5.53%	10.88%
2005	6.73%	3.12%	40.43%	−0.02%	6.49%
2006	7.34%	14.78%	18.61%	12.34%	19.21%
2007	7.18%	12.75%	36.72%	15.38%	−18.61%
2008	−23.06%	−14.95%	−35.44%	−41.41%	−55.27%
2009	19.82%	14.22%	21.58%	50.94%	17.50%
2010	3.30%	13.79%	21.78%	11.39%	11.92%
Annual Geometric Return	11.27%	11.41%	10.54%	9.39%	9.14%

Source: Lipper Inc; A Reuters Company, 1986–1998, Lipper Data, financials measured by Financial Services Funds, consumer staples by Fidelity Consumer Staples Fund, health care by Healthcare/ Biotechnology funds, energy by Natural Resources Funds, and technology by Science and Technology Funds. Return data from 1999–2008, SPDR Sector ETFs. REIT returns from the NAREIT index. Precious metals returns from Morningstar. Corporate bond data from Credit Suisse. U.S. Treasury bonds, from Ibbottson.

*Data through December 31, 2010.

TABLE 11.5 The Four Alternative Investment Components and the
Annual Returns*

Year	REITs	Investment Grade Corporate Bonds	BB-Rated Corporate Bonds	Precious Metals
1986	19.17%	16.30%	22.10%	2.05%
1987	−3.65%	1.84%	7.70%	23.76%
1988	13.47%	9.78%	13.40%	27.92%
1989	8.84%	14.12%	9.60%	38.35%
1990	−15.34%	7.37%	−0.20%	−9.07%
1991	35.69%	18.24%	27.10%	−6.13%
1992	14.58%	9.12%	12.90%	4.41%
1993	19.67%	12.43%	14.90%	−12.32%
1994	3.17%	−3.34%	−1.20%	5.29%
1995	15.25%	22.25%	20.10%	20.32%
1996	35.26%	3.28%	10.10%	33.90%
1997	20.28%	10.23%	11.90%	−14.09%
1998	−17.51%	8.57%	7.20%	−35.61%
1999	−4.62%	−1.96%	2.80%	40.89%
2000	26.36%	9.36%	3.90%	19.50%
2001	13.93%	10.31%	12.08%	2.80%
2002	3.81%	10.12%	3.47%	63.40%
2003	37.14%	8.24%	19.53%	57.20%
2004	31.59%	5.39%	9.39%	−8.20%
2005	12.17%	1.69%	2.89%	30.80%
2006	35.06%	4.30%	7.67%	31.60%
2007	−14.70%	4.56%	3.05%	23.20%
2008	−39.60%	−4.94%	−17.26%	−27.65%
2009	27.45%	18.68%	45.93%	48.48%
2010	27.58%	9.00%	13.94%	41.56%
Annual Return	10.78%	8.34%	9.98%	11.64%

Source: Lipper Inc; A Reuters Company, 1986–1998, Lipper Data, financials measured by Financial Services Funds, consumer staples by Fidelity Consumer Staples Fund, health care by Healthcare/Biotechnology funds, energy by Natural Resources Funds, and technology by Science and Technology Funds. Return data from 1999–2008, SPDR Sector ETFs. REIT returns from the NAREIT index. Precious metals returns from Morningstar. Corporate bond data from Credit Suisse. U.S. Treasury bonds, from Ibbottson.

*Data through December 31, 2010.

that typical asset allocation is counterproductive. In an attempt to lower risk and garner superior returns, pundits add international stocks. International stocks do not provide an enhanced return over the U.S. markets and have also demonstrated a strong correlation, which reduces the attractiveness of the asset. International stocks can add value only when a portfolio is positioned by sector weight. The only method to avoid a down market within traditional asset allocation is to add a significant portion of Treasury bonds. This does limit the impact of a bear market and decreases the portfolio's long-term volatility. However, since Treasury bonds also have subpar long-term returns, the process of classic asset allocation will only dilute an investor's gains. In my mind, these arcane models are a waste of time. Only by examining the markets in a different light can you attempt to secure true diversification.

The unique allocations promoted in this book give you the opportunity for outstanding investment returns with less risk. Instead of simply investing in the S&P 500 and Treasury bonds, you are siphoning out the stocks and bonds that have both high returns and low cross-correlations. Combined with my favored alternative component suggestions, such as precious metals and REITs, these portfolio allocations are the true path to a high-return, low-risk portfolio.

Both pension funds and individual investors seeking the expected return goal of 8% cannot rely on traditional asset allocation measures. In Chapter 1, I examined the history of the stock and bond markets. I projected a range of return for the coming decade based on current valuations and historical analysis of 5% to 6% (for a 50% stocks, 50% bond portfolio). This return range was based on the current price/earnings, dividend yield, and profit margin assumptions of the market in 2011. It was also based on the low intrinsic yields of Treasury bonds. Given that we can historically expect a 2–3% return above the traditional allocation using the strategies promoted in this book, meeting a 7% to 8% return hurdle is a more likely outcome. Although this return could potentially be below the needed or assumed return of most pension plans and investors, the strategy promoted in this text provides the best potential opportunity to maintain a portfolio growth rate that is better than experienced by the average investor.

Endnotes

Chapter 1

1. Using the S&P High Grade Corporate Index from 1930 to 1968, the Citigroup High Grade Index from 1969 to 1972, the Lehman Brothers U.S. Long Credit AA Index from 1973 to 1975, and the Barclays U.S. Aggregate Bond Index thereafter.

2. Harney, Matthew and Edward Tower. "Rational Pessimism: Predicting Equity Returns using Tobin's q and Price/Earnings Ratios," *Journal of Investing*, January 2003.

3. Hall, R. E. "The Stock Market and Capital Accumulation," *American Economic Review* 91, 1185–1202, 2001.

4. Liu, Laura Xiaolei and Erica X. N. Li. "Intangible Assets and Cross-Sectional Stock Returns: Evidence from Structural Estimation," Working Paper, August 2010.

5. Source: PMFA, Standard & Poor's Compustat, Federal Reserve. 2011.

6. Blackrock Corp. "Can Investors Continue to Profit from Corporate Margins," A Publication of the BlackRock Investment Institute, July 2011, https://www2.blackrock.com/webcore/litService/search/getDocument.seam?venue=PUB_IND&source=GLOBAL&contentId=1111144794.

7. Fama, E. and K. French. "Disappearing Dividends: Changing Firm Characteristics or Lower Propensity to Pay?" *Journal of Financial Economics* 60, 3–43, 2001.

8. Campbell, John Y. and Robert J. Shiller. "Valuation Ratios and the Long-Run Stock Market Outlook," *Journal of Portfolio Management*, 24: 2, 11–26, 1998.

9. Cochrane, John H. 2008. "Is Now the Time to Buy Stocks?," *Wall Street Journal*, November 12, A19. http://online.wsj .com/article/SB122645226692719401.html

Chapter 2

1. Solnik, Bruno. "Why Not Diversify Internationally Rather Than Domestically?," *Financial Analysts Journal*, July/ August 1974.
2. Lessard, Donald. "World, National, and Industry Factors in Equity Returns," *Journal of Finance* 24: 379–91. (1976). "World, Country, and Industry Relationships in Equity Returns," *Financial Analysts Journal* 32: 2–8, 1974.
3. Cavaglia, S., C. Brightman, and M. Aked (2000). On the increasing importance of industry factors: Implications for global portfolio management. *Financial Analysts Journal*, 56(5): 41–54.
4. LaBarge, Karin Peterson, 2008. "Diversification by Country and Global Sector: Considerations for Portfolio Construction," Valley Forge, PA: *Investment Counseling & Research*, The Vanguard Group.
5. West, Andrew. "International Markets Handle American Political Risk" *Capitalism Magazine*, November 13, 2000.
6. Bernstein, Richard and Kari Pinkernell. "Updated: 'Uncorrelated' Assets are Now Correlated," *Merrill Lynch Investment Strategy.* March 5, 2007.
7. Blitz, David and Pim Van Vliet. "The Volatility Effect: Lower Risk without Lower Return (April 2007)," *Journal of Portfolio Management*, 102–113, Fall 2007.
8. Thomas, Ric and Robert Shapiro. "Managed Volatility: A New Approach to Equity Investing," *The Journal of Investing*, Spring 2009.

9. Conover, C. M., G. R., Jensen, R. R. Johnson, and J. M. Mercer. "Sector Rotation and Monetary Conditions," *Journal of Investing*, 17, 34–46, 2008.

Chapter 3

1. Fogel R. W. 2008. "Forecasting the Cost of U.S. Health Care in 2040." National Bureau of Economic Research (NBER) Working Paper 14361.

Chapter 4

1. Jennings, William. "Energy Stocks as a Separate Portfolio Allocation," White Paper, 2010, www.southwestern finance.org/conf-2011/swfa2011_submission_115.pdf.
2. Chen, Peng and Joseph Pinsky. "Invest in Direct Energy," *The Journal of Investing*, 12(2):6471, Summer 2002.

Chapter 5

1. Sources: IMF World Economic Outlook; Bureau of Economic Analysis.
2. "Scary New Rich" *Newsweek*, March 6, 2010.

Chapter 8

1. Brinson, Gary P., L. Randolph Hood, and Gilbert L. Beebower, "Determinants of Portfolio Preference," *Financial Analysts Journal*, 42(4), 39–4, 1986.
2. Brinson, Gary P., Brian D. Singer, and Gilbert L. Beebower, "Determinants of Portfolio Performance II: An Update," *Financial Analysts Journal*, May/June, 1991.

3. Kozhemiakin, A. "The Risk Premium of Corporate Bonds." *The Journal of Portfolio Management*, 101–109, 2007.

4. Huang, Jing-zhi and Ming Huang, "How Much of the Corporate-Treasury Yield Spread Is Due to Credit Risk?," New York University Working Paper No. FIN-02-04, October 2002.

5. Geske, Robert L. and Gordon Delianedis. "The Components of Corporate Credit Spreads: Default, Recovery, Taxes, Jumps, Liquidity, and Market Factors." UCLA Anderson Working Paper NO. 22–01, December 2001.

6. Kealhofer, S., S. Kwok, and W. Weng. "Uses and Abuses of Bond Default Rates." CreditMetrics Monitor Publication, J.P. Morgan, First Quarter, 1998, p. 45.

7. Houweling, Patrick, Albert Mentink, and Ton Vorst. "Comparing Possible Proxies of Corporate Bond Liquidity," *Journal of Banking and Finance* 29, 1,331–1,358, 2005.

8. Williams, Rob. "Should You Worry About Bond Funds If Interest Rates Rise?," Schwab Center for Financial Research, February 24, 2010.

Chapter 9

1. "The Importance of Dividends," Northern Trust Value Investors (2008).

Chapter 10

1. De Bondt, Werner F. M. and Richard H. Thaler. "Further Evidence of Investor Overreaction and Stock Market Seasonality," *Journal of Finance* 42, 557–581, 1987.

2. Dissanaike, G. "Do Stock Market Investors Overreact?," *Journal of Business Finance and Accounting*, 24, 27–47, 1997.

About the Author

Timothy J. McIntosh is the chief investment officer of Strategic Investment Partners LLC and its affiliate, SIPCO. Mr. McIntosh holds a Bachelor of Science degree in economics from Florida State University. He has also attained a Master of Business Administration (MBA) degree from the University of Sarasota/Argosy and a Master of Public Health (MPH) degree from the University of South Florida. He is a certified financial planner (CFP) and a CFA Level II Candidate.

Mr. McIntosh served as an adjunct finance professor at Eckerd College from 1998 to 2008. He has been featured in the *Wall Street Journal,* the *New York Times, USA Today, Investment Advisor, Fortune, Barron's,* and the *St. Petersburg Times.* He was named one of the top investment advisors in the country for doctors by *Medical Economics Magazine* in 2004, 2006, 2008, 2010, and 2011. He and his wife, Kim, have two sons and reside in Boerne, Texas.

Index

Interest rates, 23–28, 127–128
　financial sector investments and, 127–128
　returns, effects on, 23–28
International investing, 32–37
International stock index (EAFE), 33–34
Internet industry, investment in, 117–119
Intrinsic valuation, 182–183
Investment guidelines, 66, 82–83, 99–100,
　　120, 138
　consumer staples sector, 99–100
　energy sector, 82–83
　financials sector, 138
　health care sector, 66
　technology sector, 120

John Hancock Financial Industries Fund
　　(FIDIX), 193

Long-term debt-to-equity ratio, 166–167
Low-volatility stocks, 39

Market cycle, 44–46
　early recession, 46
　early recovery, 45
　late recession, 45
　late recovery, 45–46
　utilization of sectors, 44–46
Medical device industry, investment in, 59–62
Milliman study, 5–6
Morgan Stanley U.S. Real Estate Fund (MSUSX),
　　195
Mutual funds, 191–194
　Fidelity Consumer Staples Fund (FDFAX),
　　192–193
　investment selection of, 191–194
　Northern Technology Fund (NTCHX), 193–194
　T. Rowe Price Financial Fund (PSIRX), 193
　Vanguard Energy Fund (VGENX), 194
　Vanguard Health Care Fund (VGHCX), 194

NASDAQ exchange, 107
Net profit margin, 169
Northern Technology Fund (NTCHX), 193–194

Oil and gas industry, 78–82
　drilling, 80–81
　energy sector investment analysis of, 78–82
　exploration and production, 81–82
　integration of, 78–79
　refining and marketing, 81–82
　services, 78–80
Operating profit margin, 169
Oppenheimer Corporate Bond Fund (OFIAX),
　　195

P/E ratio, see Price-to-earnings (P/E) ratio
Pharmaceutical industry, investment in, 57–59
Portfolio examples, 198–200. *See also* Asset
　　allocation
Price-to-earnings (P/E) ratio, 7–14, 24–28,
　　170–171
　company growth rates for, 9–12
　formula for, 8

fundamental analysis using, 170–171
　importance of, 7–9
　interest rates affects on, 24–28
　subsequent returns and, 12–14
Price-to-earning-to-growth (PEG) ratio, 172–173
Price-to-sales (P/S) ratio, 171–172
Product reliability, consumer staples sector,
　　92–93
Profit growth consistency, consumer staples
　　sector and, 90–91
Profit margin analysis,17–18, 168–170
　corporate, 17–18
　income statement calculations, 168–170
Prudential Short-Term Corporate Fund
　　(PBSMX), 195

Q ratio, 14–16
Quick ratio, 165–166

Real estate investment trusts (REITS), 157–159,
　　195
　Fidelity Real Estate Investment (FRESX), 195
　investment in, 157–159
　investment selection of, 195
Relative valuation, 182–183
Retailing industry, investment in, 93–94
Return on assets (R.O.A.), 173
Return on equity (R.O.E.), 173–174
Returns, 5–28, 32–37, 201–208
　AAII Asset Allocation Survey, 6–7
　asset allocation expectations, 201–208
　bond yields, importance of, 22–23
　corporate profit margin analysis, 17–18
　correlation of, 32–37
　dividends, importance of, 18–22
　earnings per share (E.P.S.) growth rate,
　　26–28,
　Family Office Exchange (FOX) survey results,
　　5–7
　forecasting results, 7–23
　inflation impact on, 20–22
　interest rates affects on, 23–28
　Milliman study, 5–6
　price-to-earnings (P/E) ratio, 7–14, 24–28
　Q ratio, 14–16
　Schiller P/E method, 16–17
　seven-year, 20–22
　Standard and Poor (S&P) 500 Index, 6

Schiller P/E method, 16–17
Sector allocations, 29–51
　basic materials, 42
　beta statistic, 37–41
　Brinson Partners studies, 30–31
　consumer discretionary, 42
　consumer staples, 42–43
　correlation of returns and, 32–37
　energy, 43
　financials, 43–44
　Goldman Sachs research, 31–32
　health care, 43
　industrial, 43
　international investing, 32–37